MY NAME IS ANNE, *She Said*, ANNE FRANK

JACQUELINE VAN MAARSEN was born in 1929 in Amsterdam, where she still lives. Since 1986 she has been lecturing on Anne Frank, and on discrimination, in schools all over the world. She is also the author of *Anne Frank's Heritage*.

MY NAME IS ANNE,
She Said, ANNE FRANK

Jacqueline van Maarsen

Translated from the Dutch by
Hester Velmans

ARCADIA BOOKS

Arcadia Books Ltd
15–16 Nassau Street
London W1W 7AB

www.arcadiabooks.co.uk

First published as *Ik heet Anne, zei ze, Anne Frank* by Cossee, Amsterdam, 2003

Copyright © Jacqueline van Maarsen, 2003
First published in United Kingdom by Arcadia Books, 2007
This B-format edition published 2008
This English translation © Hester Velmans, 2007

Jacqueline van Maarsen has asserted her moral right to be identified as the author
of this work in accordance with the Copyright, Designs and Patents Act, 1988.

A catalogue record for this book is available from the British Library

ISBN 978-1-905147-42-7

Printed in Finland by WS Bookwell

Arcadia Books Ltd gratefully acknowledges the financial support of the
Foundation for the Production and Translation of Dutch Literature in assisting
with the translation of this novel.

Arcadia Books supports English PEN, the fellowship of writers who work together
to promote literature and its understanding. English PEN upholds writers'
freedoms in Britain and around the world, challenging political and cultural limits
on free expression. To find out more, visit www.englishpen.org, or contact
English PEN, 6–8 Amwell Street, London EC1R 1UQ.

Arcadia Books distributors are as follows:

in the UK and elsewhere in Europe:
Turnaround Publishers Services
Unit 3, Olympia Trading Estate
Coburg Road
London N22 6TZ

in the USA and Canada:
Independent Publishers Group
814 N. Franklin Street
Chicago, IL 60610

in Australia:
Tower Books
PO Box 213
Brookvale, NSW 2100

in New Zealand:
Addenda
Box 78224
Grey Lynn
Auckland

in South Africa:
Quartet Sales and Marketing
PO Box 1218
Northcliffe
Johannesburg 2115

Arcadia Books is the *Sunday Times* Small Publisher of the Year

For Bas, Raoul, Abel, Emiel, Daan and Job,
my grandsons, and for Lili,
my granddaughter

PART ONE

Eline

1

The square in front of the train station was enormous. That she had not expected. It spread out in every direction; a river ran through it. On the periphery, the horizon was demarcated by buildings; on the far right was the tall green dome of a church. Above it all she beheld an exceptionally beautiful cloudy sky, shot with various tints of grey and here and there a tinge of blue.

It was only then that she noticed the hustle and bustle of the city, the people, the pedestrians in a hurry, a newspaper boy shouting something she did not understand. Trams were running back and forth. As they rolled up, young men armed with gunnysacks dashed to the mailboxes at the rear to empty them.

There was a stiff wind blowing. She put her valise down on the ground beside her and jammed her hatpin more firmly into her hat. Just then the sun broke through, and she was blinded for a moment by the glittering waves rippling the water before her. That was why she did not notice the young woman approaching her until the girl spoke.

'Madame Eline?' she enquired. Not waiting for the affirmative, she added in French, 'I am Bella, your assistant. I have come to pick you up.'

Bella hailed a taxi. The porter who had followed Eline with a large suitcase lifted it into the trunk.

Sweet girl, Eline thought, and fortunately she speaks French. But those grubby cotton stockings! And how poorly dressed they were, the people she saw around here! Shapeless, dull. Ugly shoes. *Quelle horreur.* What was she doing here?

'Is that a canal?' she asked Bella as they joined the traffic crossing the bridge leading into the city. Bella explained that it was part of the waters of the IJ, and that the railway station was built on an artificial island in the middle of Amsterdam's harbour.

But Eline's attention was already elsewhere, drawn by a cart decorated with little flags on the far side of the bridge, where she saw two men standing with their heads tilted back, slurping down a fish they held by the tail.

Bella followed her gaze. 'Raw herring, that's the way they eat it here,' she said.

What a peculiar custom, thought Eline.

As she listened to Bella going over some of the details of the job awaiting her, they drove through a narrow street lined with fancy shops. The people she saw walking here were well dressed. It occurred to her that these were her future customers. A limousine driver was holding open the door for a stylishly dressed lady.

They crossed three bridges. On either side, narrow strips of water.

'Those are the canals,' said Bella. Her detailed explanation of how Amsterdam was laid out, with its concentric rings of canals, went right over Eline's head.

They arrived at another square. 'Look, there's the City Theatre,' said Bella, 'and you'll be working in that building over there, on your left. This is where we turn

4

right, into Marnix Street; we have rented a couple of rooms for you there. It's just a three-minute walk from your work.'

Suddenly Eline noticed a poster advertising Yvette Guilbert, whom she had heard singing just a few months ago in one of Paris's *café-chantants*, where Maurice Chevalier was also a regular. The glimpse of Amsterdam's nightlife suddenly put her in a better mood.

As she was leaving, Bella said, 'Monsieur Robert and his wife will pick you up at seven-thirty. They are taking you to dinner at Dikker en Thijs.'

The widow renting out the rooms welcomed her in French and showed her to her two-room suite.

'I always eat early,' said the woman, 'so you may use the kitchen when you get home from work.'

'Oh, I never cook,' said Eline much to her landlady's astonishment, 'I can't cook at all. In Paris I always dine in restaurants, or I may go over to my mother's for dinner. Occasionally I'll make a pot of soup, *une bonne soupe*. Making coffee, that's all I'm good at. I've brought along my own coffee, by the way, because I heard you people are in the habit of putting something else in the coffee, and that doesn't appeal to me at all!'

'Oh, I can make you a coffee without Buisman's,'* said the woman, laughing. 'But I'll leave you now, so you can have a rest, after your journey.'

'I'm not at all tired,' said Eline. 'Why don't you make us both a cup of coffee? We can have a nice little chat.'

She took off her hat and inspected her shoes. The leather of one had been scratched on the steep kerb. She promptly

*A coffee flavour-enhancer.

kicked off both shoes and tossed them into the wastebasket, then padded into the kitchen in stockinged feet.

'How long has it been since your husband died? And do tell me, what's the matter with your leg?' she asked. The woman had trouble walking.

They discussed all the stages of the husband's illness. When they had finished, Eline asked for an ironing board and went to her room to freshen up. 'Mind that you never let them operate on your knee,' she threw in, 'I know someone who had surgery done and couldn't walk at all afterwards.'

She took the dress she intended to wear that evening from her suitcase and brought it into the kitchen, where the landlady had set up the ironing board for her, with two irons. One of the irons was already heating up on the stove.

That evening, over dinner, she gave her hosts a report of her journey.

'In Paris you told me that they all speak French here,' she said to Monsieur Robert, 'but in Brussels a group of men entered my train compartment and I couldn't understand them, or they me.'

Her boss laughed.

'Laugh all you want,' she said, offended, 'but it did mean that I had no one to talk to, and I couldn't read either, with all the commotion! I thought it very rude of them, but when the train stopped here, one of them told me, in a rather odd French dialect, *'Ceci, c'est la gare centrale d'Amsterdam,'* and said he wanted to help me with my luggage. I thought it rather fresh of him. I turned down his offer, I called for a porter.'

'Let me reassure you,' he said, 'that all our clients do speak French, as do the salesgirls who will be working for you. If you need to communicate with the girls in the workshop, Bella will be your interpreter.'

'It's good that you did not accept that man's advances,' said his wife. 'He probably thought he might get lucky with a Parisienne travelling alone!'

She enquired how Eline liked her lodgings in the bustling Marnix Street. She had chosen the place herself, together with Bella, for the view – from the front room you could see the stage entrance of the City Theatre.

'*Très confortable,*' replied Eline, and she thanked them for the trouble they had taken over it. 'But the mirror on the inside of the linen cupboard is on the small side,' she added.

She did not mention that she thought the furniture hideous, dark and heavy.

Monsieur Robert got down to business over the main course. Together they went over what her job would be: to run the haute couture department and put together a collection. For this last she would have to travel to Paris frequently. He had already briefed her on all of this, but apparently he thought it necessary to go over the whole thing once more.

He and his partner had needed all their powers of persuasion to convince Eline to accept their proposal to come to Amsterdam. The two partners went on frequent buying trips to Paris; their salon specialised in garments of the highest quality for women and children, as well as the finest fabrics for house and home. There was a ladies' tailoring department on the second floor of their building, just like the ones in Paris's couture houses. The two partners used to visit the Paris couturier where Eline worked, and she had caught their attention. They had asked her to come and work for them.

At first Eline had had no interest in going to Amsterdam. It would mean leaving her beloved Paris to move to a strange city, in a foreign country whose language she did not know, and where it was constantly raining. But the salary she was being offered was hard to resist. She had recently bought a house for her parents and her bank account could use a little topping up.

She set out for Amsterdam in a brand new Burberry raincoat, with the intention of staying for just three months.

2

Paris was the capital of the fashion world. The city's haute couture was famous for its elegant cut and sumptuous fabrics. During those ten years of euphoria, when the First World War was over and the crisis years following the stock market crash of 1929 had not yet begun, every new season would see wealthy women from all over France and from abroad flock to the Paris fashion houses to refresh their wardrobes and to order their outfits for the season's social whirl. The names on the fashion designers' marquees were known throughout the world.

When she was a little girl, Eline would wait out in the street for the big doors to swing open so that she could catch a glimpse of the cavernous hall inside. Gilded mirrors and framed fashion prints hung on walls upholstered in red velvet and gold trim. Antique chairs and étagères hugged the walls. Plush carpets covered the floors and a magnificently sparkling crystal chandelier was suspended from the ceiling. Surely this was just a foretaste of what the salons on the first floor must be like, the destination of the elegant ladies, sometimes accompanied by well-dressed gentlemen, whom she saw going in and out and who were shown upstairs by the lift boys. Once there, seated in comfortable Louis Quinze armchairs, they watched the girls modelling the latest designs parading by. The customers would pick and choose from these, assisted by a lady just as stylish as themselves: the *vendeuse*.

This haute couture fairyland was the place where, from an early age, Eline's ambitions lay. Her dearest wish was to be trained to become a *vendeuse* at one of the famous fashion houses. But her father wouldn't hear of it. He had quite another idea for his daughter's future. She was sent to a good preparatory school that would lead to a university education, and it never occurred to Eline to go against his wishes. She had great respect and admiration for her father and was therefore content to follow the path he had mapped out for her.

She was born in Paris, but her parents came from the south of France. Her grandfather had been a winegrower. He had seen his vineyards, which had been in the family for generations, wiped out in a single season, when the phylloxera blight had infested the entire region. Later, disease-resistant species from America were planted, and once the French varieties were immunised, the vineyards eventually returned to their former glory. But her grandfather did not live to see that day. He was found dead in his bankrupt vineyard, his hunting rifle at his side. Sunstroke, according to the family.

The loss of the vineyard had been reason enough for Eline's father to leave his native village. He had found employment with the Paris constabulary and had married his childhood sweetheart.

They had three children. Eline was the eldest. Her mother adored the bustle and distractions of Paris and she adjusted well to their new life. She soon made friends with many of her neighbours. When her husband worked the night shift he would sleep during the day, and so as not to disturb him, she would take the children out for a stroll, and they would explore the streets of Paris. The streets lay broken up all over the place: the Métro was being built. Eline thought the floral designs of the wrought-iron decorations over the Métro entrances were just beautiful. It was the dawning of the art nouveau movement, a new artistic style scornfully referred to as 'le style Métro'. And they would walk to the Eiffel Tower, which was just beginning to grow on the people of Paris, who really hadn't seen what was so special about it when the three-hundred-metre-tall steel edifice was under construction; but now they gloried in the fact that architects from all over the world were coming to Paris to admire the structure.

The pleasure her father took in Paris was of quite a different order. Her mother found out that he had a mistress.

She packed up and left for her parental home with her three children the very next day. Eline knew nothing of her parents' marital difficulties; her mother merely told her that they were going back to her native village for the sake of the children's health.

But she had found it a little strange that in the train her normally talkative mother had sat staring out the window in silence. Eline was kept busy looking after the little ones, so that her mother would not be disturbed in her brooding. They were on that train for hours, on their way to grandparents Eline had never seen. The last leg of the journey was by horse and buggy through rolling hills and fields of blue.

Her mother's face cleared as they rode through the familiar landscape. She sniffed in deeply the scent of the blooming lavender. Suddenly she cried out, 'We're here! Look, there's the house!'

Little Albert and Yvette, who had nodded off, woke up.

Through the trees, at the top of a hill, they spied the big house. It was known in the neighbourhood as the Commanderie. It was built of rough stone and consisted of a number of linked structures. The original part, including a chapel built centuries earlier by the Knights of the Order of Templar, was still clearly distinguishable, even though both the Hundred Year's War and the French Revolution had left their mark here. Eline saw the dovecote at the entrance that her mother had told her about, the *colombier*.

They were welcomed with open arms. There was grenadine syrup to drink, poured from a large crystal carafe. The twin uncles, who still lived at home, took Eline and her little brother and sister to the stables, where they gave them turns riding one of the horses.

Later the children met two more aunts and an uncle, who came over with their spouses and children as soon as they heard that the sister who had been so far away, for so long, had come home. The children did not meet the other six brothers and sisters. They had all taken vows as priests or nuns and were scattered around the country. They had pledged their lives to the church.

The whole family gathered around the long table on the terrace, in the shadow of an old lime tree. Friends and neighbours came over to greet them. There was much loud talking and laughter. The women brought large platters of steaming food to the table. The men poured the wine and cut hunks of brown bread from big round loaves which they held clamped close to their chests.

In the following weeks Eline would ask from time to time when they were going home again, but she never received a satisfactory answer. Nor did she understand why the pastor came to visit so often.

Six weeks later, her father came to fetch his wife and children. Eline did not hear until later that he had sworn eternal fidelity to his wife. They were sent off with the crystal carafe and the matching set of glasses.

Eline was never to see her grandparents again. A year after their daughter's visit they died within a short time of each other. The Commanderie and the vineyards were sold. Half of the proceeds went to the church. Even though the remainder of the estate had to be divided six ways, it was still a nice sum for a young family to have thrown in its lap.

For a short time it seemed that peace had returned to the family. But it was not that simple. After a while her father resumed his footloose-and-fancy-free life with his mistress while spending his wife's inheritance – the law gave him free rein to dispose of it as he liked. Eline's mother now turned a blind eye to his infidelities. She wanted her children to grow up in a harmonious atmosphere, and she simply transferred her love for her spouse to her children. She did, however, tell her eldest daughter about her father's escapades.

The respect and admiration Eline had always had for her father promptly evaporated. She decided to punish him. She quit school at once and applied for a job at one of the famous fashion houses. They took her on.

Her father was not happy about the sort of work she had to do there. She was sent out on errands, and at the end of the day she had to go around with a magnet to pick up the pins that were strewn all over the tables and floor in the workshop. She fabricated shallow rectangular boxes out of cardboard by folding up the edges, and pleated tissue paper to be layered in between the garments, so that the pricey materials would not crease when packed up and sent out. Occasionally they would let her stitch a little rolled hem. Proudly she brought her mother her first earnings. The violin, that instrument of torture which her father had insisted that she practise every day, remained where it was, hanging on the wall; she would never touch it again.

Her career soon took off; she knew how to distinguish herself in everything she did. It had started with the very first rolled hem.

Getting ahead in her career became her greatest ambition.

During the war she went to live in London for a year, to learn English. There she worked in a fashion house on Oxford Street. Even though she was terribly homesick for Paris, she stuck it out and finished her apprenticeship.

On her return she heard from her parents that her brother Albert was in hospital. He had been unable to fulfill his father's plans for him. He had left the seminary the moment it became clear that he was not in the least cut out for the priesthood, and when the war broke out he had enlisted in the army 'for the glory of the fatherland'. Alsace-Lorraine, the territory ceded to Germany in the war of 1870, had to be recaptured and returned to France. That was the reason for France's optimistic entry into this war, which everybody assumed would be over in a few months.

But the Germans started using poison gas, which seeped into the trenches, contaminating the food and water. Those who were unable to escape the asphyxiating cloud inhaled the toxic air, which attacked the eyes, throat and chest, and led to terrible retching and coughing. The soldiers panicked, scurrying every which way, trying to reach safety; but many of them succumbed and died.

Albert was lucky. He lived to tell his sister Eline about it when she visited him in hospital. After that he never spoke of it again. For him the war was over. The adventure left him with weak lungs for the rest of his days. The family nevertheless took great pride in his '*Croix de Guerre*,' the Cross of War, with which he was decorated in 1919.

He was married shortly after the war, and found a job in a department store. Eline's sister Yvette also married at a young age.

Eline had no thought of marriage. She had turned into a chic young woman and she put her career first. She was soon promoted to supervisor at the concern where she had started out as the most junior drudge. Thanks to her knowledge of English she was able to assist the foreign customers who were flocking to Paris in droves. The 'gay twenties' had begun.

Then her father's mistress died. The only reason her parents' marriage had survived was because her mother had resigned herself to not being the only woman in her husband's life. She had remained as kind and cheerful as ever, turning for companionship to her friends and acquaintances, who were all extremely fond of her.

Eline's father suddenly lost interest in everything. His career, which had initially been quite successful, ground to a halt. He was washed up, an old man before his time. His wife, always upbeat, did her best to cheer him up, but nothing helped.

Suddenly he decided that he wanted to go and live in the countryside. Eline's mother, who was so in her element in Paris, wouldn't hear of it at first. They talked it over with Eline.

Eline immediately took charge. She took her mother aside, upon which the latter agreed to move out of the city, but only on condition that from her house she'd be able to see the Eiffel Tower, and that there would be a chicken coop in the yard.

Thirty kilometres northwest of Paris there was a small

village nestled high against wooded hills, with a sweeping view of the countryside. The skyline of Paris loomed on the horizon, and the Eiffel Tower was clearly silhouetted against the clear blue sky. It was a very old parish. The church dated back to the sixteenth century, and although Gothic in style, its Renaissance influence was instantly recognisable. It was home to two sixteenth-century wooden statues. For centuries the village population had consisted largely of farmers, who passed on from father to son the cultivation of the fields lying below the village.

It was in this hamlet that Eline bought her parents a house. It had a wrought-iron fence, and stone steps leading to a terrace; in a corner of the terrace was a roomy aviary that could easily be turned into a chicken coop. Thus the house satisfied both of the conditions her mother had set.

Her parents moved, and soon settled in. It did not take long for her mother to know everyone in the village, and everyone in turn soon knew her.

During the day her father generally pottered about the house or worked in the vegetable garden at the far end of the property. When Eline visited her parents, she'd often see him out on the terrace, gazing at Paris through a telescope.

They were overjoyed when they found out they were now grandparents. Yvette had had a son.

3

After dinner, over coffee, Monsieur Robert said to Eline, 'My partner and I expect great things of you. Our business has been booming since the war, and you are the linchpin in our goal to become a world-class outfit on a level with the premier fashion houses of Paris or Brussels.'

Eline confidently replied that she was sure she would be able to live up to those expectations.

Once back in her rooms, she dashed off a letter to her parents informing them she had arrived safe and sound. She would slip it into one of those tram mailboxes tomorrow, so that they would get it without delay.

'Oh Eline, what are you going to do there, among the cows?' her father had said when she had told him about her new job in Amsterdam. 'And what kind of language do they speak over there, anyway?'

Eline had explained that the fashion house where she would be working catered exclusively to the nobility and the bourgeoisie, and that she had been assured that everyone spoke French.

He had grumbled a bit more, since she had presented him with a fait accompli, having discussed her plans with her mother but not with him. But he knew that his daughter was long past the point of asking for his consent or advice in any decision she made.

The next morning Bella came to pick her up. From the outside, the imposing building they had passed in the taxi the day before had already exceeded her expectations. But the interior too could easily compete with the fashion houses of Paris. Crystal chandeliers lit the centre hall, where hats, purses and other accessories were displayed in glass cases. Looking up, you could see the galleries of the five floors above around the perimeter of this hall.

Monsieur Robert came forward to greet Eline. 'What do you think of it?' he asked proudly.

'A real palace,' Eline responded elatedly, 'and that café, *très élégant.*'

He told her that the café usually had a band that played during the fashion shows. Eline nodded approvingly.

On her very first days on the job, she showed her skill at salesmanship not only by bringing in large clothing orders, but also by selling two Persian rugs that had been left on consignment, right off the floors of the salon. And she succeeded in talking her co-workers into switching to silk stockings, in order to improve their image. Her self-confident manner and outgoing personality helped to convince everyone that she must be right. The seamstresses were given new positions at the long tables, and four new sewing machines, with the very latest technological advances, were purchased. The only thing that mattered to her was that the work be done well.

She was ready with advice and help for Bella, who had just broken up with a boyfriend. Bella adored her new boss, and copied her in everything she did. When one night she came to Marnix Street to cry on Eline's shoulder, Eline persuaded her that no man was worth ruining her pretty little face with tears.

Yet even Bella refused one evening to deliver a gown after the drivers had gone home. The gown was to be worn that night, but none of the salesgirls felt like being seen walking down the street carrying a large box with the firm's name on it, which they considered beneath their dignity. Eline had no problem with it, however. She didn't think herself too good to deliver the package, and didn't give a fig about the impression she made in doing so.

Her job was to look after the most important customers, but when one day she saw Bella and the other salesgirls recoil from two provincially-dressed women who had just stepped hesitantly through the haute couture salon's door, she welcomed them as graciously as she used to do in Paris when greeting the Vanderbilts of New York or the Rothschilds of London. It turned out they were the wife and the daughter of a provincial textile baron, and had come to Amsterdam to order a wedding gown. And they spoke perfect French. Eline waited on them for hours, giving them her best advice – advice there was no arguing with – as they picked out the designs and fabrics. They ended up ordering not only the daughter's wedding gown and the bridesmaids' dresses, but also the bride's entire trousseau and several other items for both the mother's and the daughter's wardrobes.

Her employers offered her a contract for a permanent position after just a few weeks, but Eline hesitated.

They also did what they could to entertain her in her free time. They arranged for her to be invited to a number of soirées, and one evening they took her to the Concertgebouw to hear Yvette Guilbert when the chanteuse came over from Paris to sing in the recital hall. During the intermission, they introduced her to a business acquaintance of theirs. He had worked as a fabric wholesaler in Paris for several years.

'Now there's a man I like,' Eline later confided to Monsieur Robert. He had lovely blue eyes and dark hair, and he spoke fluent French. She was visibly disappointed when she was told that he was Dutch.

On the first nice day of spring, her employers took the initiative and invited Eline to go sailing on the Zuider Zee. To her surprise, the business acquaintance came aboard as well. His name was Hijman. 'Just call me Armand,' he said, when he saw she had trouble pronouncing his name. 'That's what they used to call me in Paris.'

They were soon engaged in animated conversation. She confessed that she wasn't all that fond of boats, partly because she did not know how to swim. 'Oh, but this is a big yacht, and the weather is perfect. Nothing will happen,' he reassured her.

In the distance she saw windmills, and church steeples, and trees. They came to a little village with wooden houses. There were fishermen walking about in dark baggy trousers. The women wore brightly striped aprons tied over long, black skirts, and little white lace caps on their heads. They shared a plate of smoked eel. Hijman took a picture of Eline standing with a man and a woman dressed in traditional costume. And he bought her a watercolour of a fisherman and his wife in a boat.

After this, there were other joint outings.

It turned out that they had many interests in common. They visited museums and went to the opera. And they scoured the markets for antiques and curios. Eline also accompanied Hijman to the antiquarian book auctions he attended in order to flesh out his collection; meanwhile she acquired an interest in old books.

It wasn't part of her plan at all, but she had fallen in love.

But she returned to Paris nonetheless. It wasn't because he was Jewish, that wasn't a problem as far as she was concerned. But she was set against the idea of spending the rest of her life in the Netherlands. She did not sign the contract, and her departure from Amsterdam seemed like an escape.

While waiting to find a new job, she moved in with her parents in the village. She didn't seem to be in a hurry. She would sit on the terrace all day with some sewing project lying untouched on her lap, or with a book she did not open. She talked to her parents about Hijman. Her father had already spoken to her about the problems that might arise in a union of two such different backgrounds. He thought she had made a sensible decision to return to Paris. Her mother had her doubts, however. She could see that Eline was suffering, but she knew what her daughter was like; she wasn't one ever to go back on a decision.

Letters arrived from the Netherlands. Eline kept taking longer to reply, and after a few months the correspondence stopped.

She rented an apartment in Paris on the Avenue de Wagram, near the Champs Elysées. She returned to her previous job, and her life in Paris resumed its familiar routine, as if nothing had happened.

A few months later Hijman suddenly appeared at her door.

'We're getting married,' he said, 'I'm moving my business back to Paris.'

She looked at him, speechless.

Together they went to the village, where Eline introduced Hijman to her parents. Her mother was overjoyed to see her daughter so happy, and welcomed the pair with her usual warmth. Her father held back a little at first. He had not looked forward to meeting the man she had chosen, but he had to admit that it wasn't as bad as he'd feared, and that the two of them seemed very well suited. He saw how comfortable his future son-in-law was with French customs, and how well he had mastered the French language. Eline was happy to see that her father's prejudices were soon overcome, and that Hijman seemed quite at ease in her parents' home.

They were just in the middle of an animated conversation when her brother Albert walked in. 'Good afternoon,' he said, to show that he too could speak a foreign language. He spoke English with a heavy French accent. Eline looked at him darkly. 'I told you Armand speaks French, didn't I?' she said. Hijman couldn't help smiling.

'Where did you learn such excellent English?' he asked, upon shaking Albert's hand. Albert told him he had studied it in the seminary and that it came in very handy at La Samaritaine, the Paris department store where he worked.

Eline decided this was a good time to leave the men alone, and went into the kitchen with her mother. She had seen that her mother was impressed with her dark, handsome beau with the clear blue eyes.

'What do you think of Armand?' she asked.

'It certainly was worth it, waiting so long for the right one to come along,' her mother replied, giving Eline a big hug. 'I am sure that you'll be very happy with him.'

On their way back to the city Eline told Armand about her brother's divorce. One day, a few years earlier, she had found her parents all in a state. Her brother had for a long time suspected his wife of being unfaithful, and that morning she had left a note announcing that she had moved in with her lover for good. He had gone to his parents' house to fetch his military pistol, and had stormed out the door in a frenzy. Eline, who knew what her hot-tempered brother was capable of, had run after him, and had been just in time to stop him from committing a double murder.

There was nothing to stop them from getting married anymore. Eline did not tell her parents that she had decided to convert to Judaism. They were very much taken with their future son-in-law, but this would have been too much for her father to swallow. Armand, for his part, did not tell his parents that his favourite dish in the Paris restaurants was non-kosher lobster.

Back in Amsterdam, Armand had already taken Eline to meet his parents once, on a Friday night when the whole family gathered for dinner to see in the Sabbath. She had observed with interest the lighting of the candles, the prayer over the goblet of wine and the cutting of the braided challah bread. Armand had explained to her the symbolic meaning of these rituals.

But she did not really have much contact with his family, other than with Arie, his elder brother, who spoke fluent French, and with his younger sister Martha, whom she considered pretty, sweet and smart.

She received instruction in the Jewish religion and customs

from the rabbi in Paris. She found out that it wasn't that easy to become Jewish, however. In order to convert, besides demonstrating a sincere desire to do so, she had to become thoroughly conversant with Jewish traditions. Her training culminated in a sober marriage ceremony in the Paris synagogue.

Arie came to Paris to act as witness; Albert was the other witness. Hijman's family had conveyed that travelling to Paris would be too much for them. So Eline had told her own parents that they had decided to just have a very quiet civil wedding.

Shortly thereafter they left for a winter-sport honeymoon in the Bavarian town of Garmisch-Partenkirchen.

On their return they found her parents grief-stricken at the loss of their beloved grandson, and mystified by their youngest daughter Yvette's inexplicable deed. Her father had always expected great things of Yvette: she was pretty and very talented. But as a child she had been fond of malicious pranks, and later in life she never seemed to carry through anything that she had begun, whereas Eline, who had gone her own way against her father's wishes, had always persevered and accomplished all she set out to do.

At first Eline was at a loss as to how to console her parents, but in the end she did come up with a plan, as always. First she arranged things so that her sister was put into an institution rather than being sent to prison, an outcome the family had feared.

Next she made an important decision. She had never wanted to have children because they would interfere with her career. But her brother Albert was divorced, and it did not seem likely that there would be any more grandchildren forthcoming from Yvette's side. The only solution was for Eline to come up with some herself.

Some time later Eline and Hijman arrived at the village with glad tidings. For the first time in months, Eline saw the sadness in her mother's face lift. Her father grabbed the kerosene lamp and went down to the cellar to choose a bottle of wine. A special wine for a special day. Their future was restored to them once more. A new grandchild was on the way.

So it was that Hijman and Eline's daughter was conceived with a deliberate aim in mind. Her task was to replace her little French cousin.

4

For a full year Eline devoted herself to motherhood and domesticity. But little by little she began to miss her work. However, she did not feel like going back to her former job for a third time. She toyed with the idea of setting up her own dress shop in Amsterdam, especially since she realised that Hijman would very much like to return to his hometown.

His brother Arie had been acting as his partner, running the Amsterdam side of Hijman's business, which consisted of importing fabrics from France and England. The collaboration had been working out well, but now Arie wanted to move to the town of Santpoort, where his fiancée worked as a nurse at the psychiatric hospital. So there was a certain amount of pressure from Amsterdam for Hijman to come back.

They took a lease on a large townhouse on Willemsparkweg, dating from the end of the nineteenth century. They furnished the two parlours on either side of a marble central hall in the style of the Paris salons. The antique French furniture they had brought over from Paris had pride of place there. The suite was divided into a 'pink salon' and a 'green salon'; in each room all the carpeting, silk jacquard curtains and silk upholstery were done in the same colour. That had been Hijman's idea. Only the large green salon's leather-topped desk, displaying the pattern books and fabric swatches, betrayed the fact that this was a fashion salon. And the *miroir brot*, backed in pink silk, a three-way looking glass purchased from Paris's Maison Brot, purveyor of mirrors, was the clue that the pink salon was the fitting room. This was where Eline received her clients. Hijman's office was in a small back room on the same floor.

Mathilde, the German live-in maid, took the child for a daily walk in nearby Vondelpark. All the houses along Willemsparkweg and the surrounding streets had a basement with a large kitchen facing the street, a spacious garden room at the back, and a couple of maids' rooms. The garden room was the child's daytime domain, and it was where the meals were taken as well. After dinner Eline and Hijman would retire to the conservatory behind the salons, where they sipped tea from Sèvres porcelain cups. Hijman read the *Algemeen Handelsblad* and Eline *Le Figaro*, which was sent to her daily from Paris. And there, seated at her empire desk, Eline would write letters to her parents and her French friends. The conservatory was also where guests were received; family or very close friends were welcomed downstairs, in the garden room.

On the top floor, housing the bedrooms, a room was allocated for the workshop. It was furnished with mannequins, sewing machines and two large tables at which first four, and soon afterwards six seamstresses sat at work. They wore white aprons with long sleeves; Eline wore one of these too whenever she wasn't waiting on customers downstairs. The customers spoke French, the language then commonly used in the higher circles to which her clientele belonged.

Eline and Hijman made frequent trips to Paris, where Eline attended the fashion shows of the leading fashion houses and purchased *calques* of the designs she had chosen. These were watercolours drawn on tracing paper, which she would show to her clients in Amsterdam. The client would choose what she wanted from these; then the pattern was ordered. Next she would help her client pick out the fabrics from the Paris textile-wholesalers' books of swatches. Hijman would order the fabrics over the phone, and sometimes they were flown in by KLM the very next day. The patterns, called *toiles*, made of unbleached cotton, were draped on mannequins and adjusted to the client's size, after which the adapted pattern was transferred to the chosen fabric.

Sometimes Eline went to stay with her parents in the village, and the grandparents would babysit their grandchild in the daytime. By the time Eline and Hijman returned home in the evening, the house would be filled with the smells of French cuisine. Artichokes, mushrooms and garlic: vegetables that came fresh from the farm here, but were virtually unknown in Holland. Hijman brought cheese, cookies and chocolate from Holland, and in order to give his in-laws a sense of the Dutch landscape he bought for them some paintings, which were immediately given pride of place on the drawing-room walls. A reproduction of a painting by Nicolas Maes he had bought for his mother-in-law, of an old woman praying, hung over her bed.

Hijman and Eline's father had long talks about the political situation in Europe and about the economic crisis, so bad for business and causing so much poverty. Their mutual interest in nineteenth-century French literature – Balzac, Flaubert, Baudelaire, Zola – was also a frequent topic of conversation.

One day this led to an argument between the two men over the Dreyfus affair: the arrest of Captain Alfred Dreyfus on charges of treason, his life sentence and banishment to

Devil's Island. Captain Dreyfus had been the victim of a conspiracy by a group of senior French officers, who used a forged piece of evidence to prove his guilt. Emile Zola, in the tract *J'accuse* which he wrote as an open letter to *L'Aurore*, would eventually defy the military, church and aristocratic establishments, resulting in a reversal of the sentence and the exoneration of the captain who had been so unjustly persecuted.

Eline and her mother looked at each other. Eline knew that at the time of the affair her father, like the average Frenchman, had been for the military. It had even caused some domestic discord, since her mother's intuition had led her to believe that the officers had been motivated by anti-Semitism. Eline put an end to the touchy subject by announcing that dinner was served.

After dinner the two women would clear the plates, and on nice summer evenings they would go out to the terrace; leaning over the fence, they'd chat with the passers-by, all of them acquaintances from the village. Or they would stroll over to the neighbours' to discuss the latest piece of gossip.

A second child announced itself unexpectedly. This did not suit Eline's plans at all. Establishing her new business took up much of her energy; she took hot baths in hopes of ending her pregnancy. But it was to no avail.

In January of 1929 a second daughter was born. She turned out better than expected: unlike her sister, who demanded constant attention day and night and cried a lot, this was a calm baby, who did everything by the book.

PART TWO
Jacqueline

1

I was taken to France for the first time when I was six months old. My father and mother had to go to Paris to scout the latest high-fashion fads and to do the buying for my mother's dress shop. Since I was still being breastfed, they had to take me; my sister stayed behind in Amsterdam with our German nanny, who'd been hired when I was born. My grandparents looked after me; my mother would take the train back from the Gare Saint-Lazare every day at lunchtime in order to feed me. She took a taxi for the last leg to and from the station.

The earliest memory I have of France is of the holiday I spent there when I was two and a half. It was a total disaster. They had no idea what to do with me. I kept crying out in Dutch, 'I want my Mummy,' which is why my Uncle Albert always called me *Mamitou* for years to come.

I refused to speak French. With great difficulty my grandmother finally managed to worm the word *poupée*, doll, out of me, which I whispered in her ear. As a reward, that evening Uncle Albert brought me a beautiful doll from Paris.

My sister had no problem speaking French. For that reason she was usually the one to speak up. My parents still lived in Paris when she was born; my mother hadn't been working and used to spend the entire day with her, so French was my sister's mother tongue.

My mother made a habit of addressing me only in Dutch. I had been born in the Netherlands, and since she only saw us at night, she thought I would not be able to understand her if she spoke French to me. Even when I had begun to know some French, she would often switch to Dutch with me. It irked her to hear me make mistakes in French, and she did not try to hide her irritation. But I did understand every word, since I was used to hearing my mother speak French with my father, who possessed a fluent command of the language.

My mother had picked up just enough Dutch by this time to make herself understood. That was enough as far as she was concerned; her mastery of that language would barely improve over the years.

She often called me her 'Dutch daughter', and she would say it either ruefully or proudly, depending on whether we happened to be in France or in Holland.

Even though I relied on my sister as much as possible and spoke as little as I could get away with when we were at our grandparents' house, the weeks we spent there every summer holiday did help to improve my French. Actually, Grandmother did not mind my mistakes, but Grandfather would raise his eyebrows every so often when he heard me mangling his mother tongue. I was aware that it annoyed him, just as it did my mother. It made me feel insecure, and I realised I did not live up to his image of a proper French granddaughter.

Being a city kid, I was captivated by the life of the village. I was woken every morning by the crowing of the rooster in my grandmother's chicken coop. Instead of NO. 2 trams, here farmers' carts rumbled past the house, and from the crack of dawn I heard the drivers yelling 'giddy-up' at the horses. At the sound of hooves beneath the window, I would jump out of bed and fling open the shutters. We waved at the women in the wagons, facing each other in two rows on narrow wooden benches in their blue headscarves. They were on their way to work in the fields. They all knew who we were: the Dutch granddaughters of the 'Parisiens'.

The first thing we did was to help Grandmother feed the chickens. We cradled the freshly-laid eggs carefully in a basket; those eggs were for our breakfast. Grandmother always made redcurrant jelly with the berries from the garden; I loved this jam so much that I dolloped huge spoonfuls of it on my bread. We were served sweet *café au lait* in wide bowls; I liked to dunk my croissant in it.

It was especially in the morning, at breakfast, that I was conscious of how much Grandmother enjoyed our company for those four summer weeks when my parents had gone back to Amsterdam and she had us all to herself.

Later in the morning we'd go shopping with her. We'd have to stop and wait every so often as she exchanged the latest gossip with the other women of the village. I would stand by shyly and not say a word. But I was quite willing to let her friends kiss and pet me.

When we came home, we would find Grandfather sitting out on the terrace sipping his first glass of cognac. He'd be reading the newspaper or peering at Paris through his telescope. He let us look through it too. The Eiffel Tower suddenly seemed very close.

Once, when my parents had taken us to visit the Eiffel Tower, I asked when we got home, 'Did you see me up there, Grandfather? I waved at you.'

'Of course I saw you,' he replied, 'in your little red hat.'

Slowly but surely we were starting to have careful conversations, in which I tried my best not to make any mistakes.

Even though during those summer weeks we were within striking distance of Paris, we rarely went into the city, other than passing through on our arrival and departure. We did once stay a little longer with Uncle Albert; it was the only time we spent Christmas in France. The reason for that visit was Princess Juliana's marriage on 7 January 1937. My mother's business had gone through a rough patch after the stock market crash of 1929; quite a few of her wealthy clients had lost everything, or at least a substantial part of their fortunes, and no longer had the wherewithal to restock their wardrobes on a regular basis. She had managed to keep the shop afloat nonetheless. But in 1937 the entire Dutch aristocracy had to be outfitted with formal attire for the royal wedding. My mother's haute couture atelier was back in full swing, with ten girls working around the clock. My mother really couldn't have her children underfoot while this was going on, and so she sent us to her parents and brother for the holiday. Uncle Albert took us to see his girlfriend Jeanne, whom he fondly called '*ma grosse*', my fat one; she treated us to pastries, and helped herself to three.

When Grandmother prepared lunch Grandfather would read to us. Since French children were raised on the books of Bécassine, the daft little girl from Brittany with the heart of gold, he was set on having his Dutch granddaughters make her acquaintance too. My grandfather's favourite Bécassine story was the one about the First World War, *Bécassine pendant la Guerre*.

He also taught us French nursery rhymes, playing the tunes on his zither for us. Some of these my mother had already taught us, like 'Frère Jacques' and 'Au clair de la lune'. Uncle

Albert had brought us a big illustrated book from Paris with all the songs in it. I always followed along carefully and learned the songs by heart. I liked those songs. I didn't know any Dutch songs like them; at school in Amsterdam all we ever learned were patriotic songs, usually something to do with the Eighty Years' War. Nor did they have anything in common with the scary rhymes and fairytales the German maid liked to regale us with, which sometimes caused me to lie awake all night.

In the afternoon we would walk out into the countryside with Grandmother, gathering the stalks left behind after the wheat was mown, which we used as chicken feed. The hard stubble pricked our legs. I loved to chew on the grains, for the sweet taste.

Many an afternoon we'd also stop at the churchyard. As time went on it began to dawn on me that there was some mystery in the family that was never mentioned, and that this secret had something to do with the cemetery at the end of my grandparents' lane. It was surrounded by a white wall and the iron gate squeaked when you opened it. In the sun-drenched churchyard I would trail along the paths between the graves, examining the yellowed photos propped on the stones and admiring the artificial flowers that decorated some of the graves. I tried to touch the lizards basking on the warm tombstones, but they always heard me approach over the gravel and would shoot into cracks and crevices as quick as a flash.

Grandmother always made straight for one particular grave. Once I knew how to read, I saw that it was inscribed *'Notre petit René'*. She would bustle about in silence with flowerpots and a watering can, and then we would leave by the squeaky gate again, without my opening my mouth. I knew instinctively that it was best not to ask any questions.

One time I did put the question to my mother. 'Who *is* that little René?' I asked.

My mother kept it short and sweet: René was the dead child of her younger sister Yvette. I had met Yvette just once, when she paid her parents a visit. She had a nickname in the family: *la folle*, the crazy one. I wouldn't get to hear the rest of the story until years later.

In the daytime we often played with the girl next door, Chantal. If only because of her, I began to look forward to the yearly stay in France more and more. We picked blackberries together along the road leading to the forest. And Chantal taught us which snails to put in our basket. Later Grandmother would dump the snails into a bucket of salt. The next day she would rinse the slimy mess thoroughly, then sprinkle it with fresh salt. She would repeat this for a few days. Then the snails were cooked with lashings of garlic. My father was especially fond of this non-kosher delicacy. But I could not bring myself to swallow it, no matter how hard I might try to please my grandfather.

My father would not let us go into the woods alone. The woods were home to quite a number of wild boar, and they were dangerous. Sometimes my grandfather would let us peer through the bistro window, to show us the trophies of the annual hunt: boar heads with bloodthirsty tongues protruding from pointy snouts. That was enough to give us the willies and refrain from going into the forest by ourselves.

My grandfather liked to talk about the annual autumn hunt. When the men of the village shot a boar, the dead animal was carted back to the village in triumph in the back of a wagon. On the first Sunday after that, the butcher would light a fire early in the morning and roast the pig on a spit. He caught the melting drippings in a metal basin and dipped rags wrapped around a long stick into the fat to baste the carcass so that the meat would turn out juicy and succulent, with a nice brown crust. After mass, the farmers' families would gather for a *déjeuner champêtre*, at which the boar was the guest of honour. Three men were needed to lift the heavy, steaming-hot roast from the spit. Then the butcher skilfully carved the meat off the bone. Everyone got his fair share. Delicious salads were provided by the women, there was bread and wine, and much animated talk and laughter; all the children of the village took part in the festivities. The boar's head would later come to hang in the bistro, over a plaque bearing the name of the bold marksman who had shot it, and the date.

Every day we would join Grandfather in the vegetable garden, where he proudly showed off his green beans. Chantal's father thought so highly of Grandfather's beans that he took them to market for him, where they went like hotcakes. Chantal's father owned most of the fields in the valley, and he came from one of the village's oldest families. He had invented a special irrigation system and his fields were always green and lush. At night big loads of his vegetables were shipped to Les Halles, Paris's wholesale vegetable market. The women I used to see sitting in the wagons that trundled by my bedroom window every morning worked in Chantal's father's fields.

On the way back from the vegetable garden, we'd walk through the orchard, where I would pick up the plums that had fallen from the trees. My father had bought several fields close to the village, and this orchard was one of the ones he had purchased. The crop from the fruit trees was also sold at the market. My father had made a deal with Chantal's father that his farmhands would look after our fruit trees.

The peaches from the big tree on the terrace were for our own consumption. They were large, juicy and sweet, and the tree was always heavily laden with fruit, no matter how much you picked.

Once a week we accompanied Chantal to the rectory in the village, where the priest organised a special afternoon for children. There we met Chantal's schoolmates. They thought we were strange, they weren't used to meeting foreign kids. My sister immediately felt at home in this group, but I sensed the others staring at me and did not feel comfortable there.

The village fair was traditionally held in August, so it always coincided with our stay. It was a small carnival with a merry-go-round and a swing in the form of a large boat that could hold up to ten children. What a treat when Uncle Albert took us there on a Sunday afternoon! He showed off his marksmanship in the shooting gallery and he let us toss as many balls as we needed to capture the teddy bear we had our hearts set on.

Every day in the late afternoon I would walk down the lane to see if Uncle Albert was on his way. The train from Paris stopped in a neighbouring town, and he walked the rest of the way home. We'd wave to each other from afar. He had grown used to this niece of his with the quirky habits. Sometimes he'd come home early and take us to the cinema in another village where they were showing films for children. It was a thirty-minute walk there and back. They were the same films my father took me to see in Amsterdam's Cineac, only here Popeye and Donald Duck spoke French instead of Dutch.

Wine was drunk at dinner. In the cellar there were two large casks, from which either Grandfather or Uncle Albert would tap a carafe. Once, when the wine had made me throw up all night long, my mother told her father that under no circumstances was he to serve wine to us any more, not even mixed with water, the way French children drank it, my sister too on occasion. 'Dutch children don't drink wine,' she told him. When he noticed that I preferred water, he grumbled, 'Water is for frogs.' Uncle Albert began making croaking noises.

But my grandfather did obey his daughter's strictures, even if with reluctance. The water from the pump was not potable. They gave me Eau de Vichy mineral water from a bottle; it tasted a bit sour, and I drank it only when I got very thirsty.

I have some happy memories, especially of summer evenings when my parents were with us. The adults sat at the table on the terrace chatting, and my father kept topping up the glasses. Blue gladiolas grew along the chicken coop. The bees buzzed in the fragrant climbing roses growing up the side of the house, and along the railing were rows of clay pots filled with geraniums blooming so abundantly that they poked their heads right out of the diamond-shaped openings. I played among the flowers and, when my mother wasn't looking, dipped my madeleine into my grandfather's wine.

Then my grandfather and I would exchange a conspiratorial glance and I fancied that he looked at me approvingly.

In 1939, at the end of the summer vacation, we said our goodbyes. '*A l'année prochaine*, see you next year,' we cried to one another.

The next April we received a telegram from Uncle Albert: *Maman décédée*, Mother deceased. I did learn a new word, but I was very sad. Nobody had told us Grandmother was ill.

My mother immediately left for the funeral and was gone for several weeks. France had been at war with Germany since September, so Albert had had to request special permission for his sister's visit.

On 9 May 1940, one day before the Germans invaded the Netherlands, she arrived back in Amsterdam on the last train.

2

I barely knew my grandparents on my father's side. My grandfather had died before I was a year old, and I don't remember much of my grandmother, who passed away when I was three. I don't think I was taken to see her very often. My mother had set up a financial support system for her mother-in-law, the brunt of which fell largely on my parents and Uncle Arie, my father's oldest brother. In hindsight I think my mother did not want to have her mother-in-law come and live with us, as was customary in those days. The family had found a way to accept Uncle Arie's Gentile wife, but my mother, who on top of everything was French and spoke a very peculiar version of Dutch, was regarded with suspicion.

This did not bother her at all. She always remained true to herself, in every way. For my father she would set the Friday-night table with a white tablecloth and candles, the way the rabbi in Paris had taught her, but beyond that she wasn't going to go out of her way to adapt to her new family. She was very fond of Aunt Martha, my father's youngest sister, who lived in Amsterdam and for whom she felt sorry because in her opinion Martha had married a *schlemiel** – a Yiddish

---

*A loser

word my mother had adopted from her Jewish relatives. In the meantime my father went to great lengths to have his wife and children registered as members of the *Nederlands Israëlitisch Kerkgenootschap*, the Netherlands Jewish Church Affiliation, at first without much success. My parents' Paris marriage was deemed too liberal to be recognised by Amsterdam's strict orthodox Jewish community.

The fact that my sister and I were also considered outsiders by our grandmother was made plain by a story my sister once told me. As was customary in those days, my father had named his eldest daughter after his mother. When my father noticed that his mother's jewellery was being handed down piece by piece to my cousin Chrisje, he asked for an explanation. 'She is my namesake,' was the answer. This infuriated my father.

'Christiane was also named after you, even if that is the French version of the name, so there's no reason to make a distinction between them.'

My sister owes my grandmother's diamond ring and gold watch to this intervention of my father's.

My father kept up a close relationship with his brothers and sisters. This meant that we saw our cousins quite a bit: four cousins in The Hague, daughters of Aunt Greta, and one in Amsterdam – Deetje, Aunt Martha's daughter.

We got along well with Aunt Greta's two youngest daughters, Betsy and Meta, who were the same age as us; we often stayed at each other's houses. I did not like sleepovers and was prone to homesickness, but when I was with my sister I didn't mind it so much. Once, when the family had come over to our house and Meta and I had had a good time playing together, Meta proposed that I return to The Hague with them and stay over a couple of days. Her enthusiasm was infectious and I said yes, but then I dreaded the thought of it and it took me quite a bit of effort to extricate myself from my promise. I had to turn to my father for help, the only one who understood. It was also because I thought Uncle Maurits wasn't a very nice man. He made us feel we were different because of my parents' mixed marriage; we did not follow Jewish traditions very strictly. He often interrogated us and made snide comments about the way we were being raised. If we then burst into tears, he would mock us. We did think Aunt Greta was sweet, but she didn't have much of a say.

Deetje was the same age as me, and we often played together from a very young age. At Aunt Martha's we celebrated the Passover Seder every year in commemoration of the Jewish people's exodus out of Egypt in the time of the pharaohs, thousands of years ago. Deetje, who went to Hebrew class, could follow the text pretty well; I just looked at the pictures. One showed a man in a long coat with outspread arms, who made the sea split in two so that the Jews could pass through freely, and once they had all reached the other side, the sea closed up again just as their pursuers were racing up. So everything turned out all right in the end.

At a certain point in the evening the front door was opened, because the prophet might come in. He never did, though.

Meanwhile we savoured the delicious vegetable soup prepared by my aunt.

At family gatherings such as these we did pick up some knowledge of the beliefs of my ancestors. Very occasionally, on special holidays, we would accompany my father to the synagogue, but in general it was not really a big part of our life.

3

On entering our Willemsparkweg house, I hardly ever climbed the stone steps up to the front door, but clambered in through the basement window instead, stepping onto the kitchen counter and then jumping down to the floor. My cup of milk would be waiting for me in the kitchen, which I'd drink before going upstairs to the workroom, to see if my mother was up there, or to potter about a bit, helping the seamstresses by picking up pins with a magnet, or stuffing fabric scraps into a big bag. It was always a cheerful to-do up there. When it was busy, everyone pitched in to get the work finished in time. The girls liked working for my mother, who showed a personal interest in each of them.

One Christmas they came up with a little tree with Christmas decorations for us when they saw that we did not have a Christmas tree. My father was not pleased, but we set it up in our own room anyway, thrilled with the glittering ornaments and candles. He turned a blind eye because he didn't want to spoil our fun.

The banister of the steep staircase in our house was a brilliant slide, and I always took advantage of it when I had to go downstairs. One day I landed with a smack at the feet of one of my mother's posh customers, who was just being shown into the salon.

'Is that your little girl? I did not know you had any children. *Elle est ravissante avec ces grands yeux bleus*,' the lady exclaimed, and began addressing me in French.

My mother, who liked to keep her business and private life strictly separate, ignored that last comment, even though it had been just such blue eyes that she had fallen for when she had met my father. She said in an irritated tone of voice, 'She doesn't speak French.'

'That's strange, even though her mother is French?'

'Not a word,' my mother added. Pulling the cap off the speaking tube connecting the middle floor with the ones above and below, she blew into the opening, making a whistling sound. A single whistle was for the workroom, two whistles meant she was calling Frolline downstairs. Frolline was the German nanny; at least that was what my mother, who did not speak German, called her, and we copied the way she pronounced the word Fräulein.

Through the tube my mother told Frolline to come and fetch me at once. But I was already bolting downstairs to the kitchen, where I allowed Frolline to console me. I realised that I had done something wrong, although I did not know exactly what. It was then that I took the decision never to speak a word of French again in my mother's presence. I would keep my vow for years.

I adored Frolline. She was always there for me throughout my baby and toddler years. My rag doll's name was Konraat, named after Frolline's fiancé, Konrad, in Düsseldorf. It was with her that we went for walks in Vondelpark and fed the ducks. It was her hand that I clutched in the Carré Theatre when Rupert Bear was cornered by the wicked witch. She read to us from *Struwelpeter*, in which naughty children were subjected to the most gruesome punishments. Although I did not understand the German nursery rhyme in which a knight who tumbles into a grave is eaten by ravens, it did make me shiver. One of the books she read to us had a picture of a sinister little fellow lying in wait under the bed, ready to stick out his hand and grab the ankle of a little boy trying to climb into bed. For the longest time I had to check under my bed before I would get into it.

The language barrier was no problem. For both Mathilde and Frolline, we had come up with a language that teetered somewhere between Dutch and German.

Some years later, when I was at school, Frolline would help out in the workroom during school hours. Our dresses were sewn for us there. We were allowed to pick out the pattern ourselves.

My sister sketched sumptuous garments that were turned into somewhat simplified models; in summer she would parade proudly down the street in her new dress. Once, when it looked like it was going to rain, she insisted on wearing her new dress to school, without a coat. There was a scuffle and quite an uproar, ending with a smart box on the ear from Frolline. All to no avail: she went out without a coat anyway. When she was halfway down the Reijnier Vinkeles Quay the skies opened up. She arrived at school soaked to the skin. Frolline had to pick her up and take her home to change her clothes.

I modelled my wardrobe after Shirley Temple and the Canadian quintuplets who were constantly in the news. At my request Frolline bought a certain brand of soap in great quantities, so that I could exchange the packaging for paper dolls of the idols who were my inspiration. My mother did not use that brand, because she always brought her own soap back from Paris. Later, during the war, when soap was hard to come by, those extra bars came in handy; we had soap in abundance until close to the end.

But suddenly Frolline was gone. At the end of the summer holidays my father picked us up from my grandparents in France. When we came home I immediately asked where she was; normally she would be waiting for us with a happy smile. 'Frolline has gone back to her own country,' said my father. 'You are too big now for a nanny. Rika will be the one to walk you to school and pick you up.'

Rika was our new maid. She came from the town of Meppel and had been Mathilde's successor when Mathilde returned to Germany.

Many Dutch families at that time had German maids; they sought employment abroad because of Germany's poor economy. But over the course of the 1930s the number of German housekeepers gradually dwindled.

In Van Eeghen Street, behind Willemsparkweg, lived a client of my mother's, an Austrian lady residing with her son and daughter-in-law. They too had a German nanny looking after their two little boys. The girl in question, Else, was engaged to a cousin of my father's. The German girls knew each other from the park, where they used to meet each other while on a stroll with their charges. But Else was under strict orders from her employer, the mother of the two little boys, not to talk to our Frolline if she had 'the seamstress's children' with her. I don't know if my mother knew about this at the time, but later, when Else had long been married to this cousin, the story invariably came up in company. My mother refused to comment, but I saw that she was greatly irked at this social snub.

Actually, Rika's arrival had touched off quite a fracas in our house. I was five years old and she arrived on the day I was rushed to hospital to have my appendix out. As Rika entered, my sister yelled, 'My little sister is in the hospital!' My parents were upset and berating each other for not having realised how serious it was and waiting too long to call the doctor, when my condition had become quite critical. It had been my own fault really, because as usual, I had put off letting them know that I wasn't feeling well. It happened on St Nicholas's Day. We had had people over, visitors who had brought us presents. I wanted to play with my new toys and was sitting quietly by the stove. It wasn't until I started vomiting that anyone paid any attention to me, and something was finally done. Rika told me later that she'd decided she could not stay in this crazy house a minute longer, and had rushed out the door. My mother, who had liked Rika very much at their first meeting, promptly went after her, found her at her fiancé's place in Amsterdam, and begged her to come back. Rika was with us for many years.

I was sad that Frolline had left and went down to Rika in the kitchen for consolation. She was making potato pancakes. I broke off a crispy piece from the stack of golden pancakes, crammed it in my mouth and went to sit on a stool next to the stove with my doll, Konraat, on my lap. Rika ladled three spoonfuls of batter into the hot oil. She looked at me quizzically.

'What's the matter?' she asked.

'I don't understand why Frolline didn't even say goodbye to us,' I pouted. 'Wasn't she even a little bit sad to leave us?'

'Hasn't your father told you anything, then?' asked Rika. I shook my head. Then she told me what had happened.

The real Konrad had talked Frolline into taking stuff from the house on a regular basis. Rika, who when cleaning the house kept finding things missing, had tipped off my father, because she didn't want to be accused of thievery herself. A few days after my mother had taken my sister and me to

Paris for our annual summer holiday, Konrad came to pick up his fiancée for a visit to the family in Düsseldorf. At the door my father insisted that she open her bulging suitcase – a pair of wicker trays tied together with a belt. In it he found a good portion of the family silver.

Frolline was fired and sent back to Germany. She had wept because she would never see us again, said Rika. It had also been hard for her to say goodbye to my mother. Her employer had entrusted her with her daughters, leaving the girls' upbringing up to her, and had always treated her with the greatest sympathy and kindness. Frolline respected and admired my mother, and she placed great store in her good opinion. My mother, who had rushed back from Paris, had advised her in no uncertain terms to dump Konrad, but whether Frolline had taken her up on that advice, Rika did not know. She did not tell us a detail I only heard later, that Frolline's fiancé was a Nazi sympathiser, another reason to have nothing to do with her any more.

I hurled Konraat into a corner of the kitchen and went to play in the street until I was called inside for dinner.

4

Hitler came to power in Germany on the day I turned four. Anti-Semitism officially became the national policy there. Slumbering feelings of anti-Semitism were fanned into flame, leading to murderous aggression. Germany's persecution of the Jews had begun.

I knew nothing of all that. For my birthday my parents presented me with the doll I had long been coveting, and my sister gave me an album to house my cigar-band collection. Frolline delighted me with a box of coloured soaps and with it a little white stone pipe for blowing bubbles.

One thing I did notice, however, was that there were a lot of new children at our school. I knew they had come from Germany, but I didn't realise they were all Jewish.

Much later, in 1938, after Kristallnacht, our classrooms at the Montessori school became overcrowded. I knew nothing of anti-Semitism and nothing at all of Kristallnacht, a word cynically coined by the Nazis who had smashed the windows of Jewish shops that night, blanketing the streets in shattered glass.

The German children were different and they spoke a foreign language, for which they were greatly mocked. The way they said hello, especially, with a handshake and a little curtsy, gave rise to much hilarity. But the children in my class who had fled Nazi Germany with their parents at a young age adapted easily, and soon learned to speak Dutch. The Montessori emphasis on independent learning was better suited to children learning a new language than traditional teaching methods.

My father took a great interest in Montessori education. The principle was to give children the opportunity to develop all the different aspects of their intelligence. The teachers were charged with giving children free rein when it came to learning, and to show them how to use the specially designed teaching materials. 'Teach me how to do it myself' was the motto. There were no report cards, so that the children would not compare themselves with each other, and they were never held back. We did not sit at school desks, we each had our own little table instead, which was quite unusual at the time. Punishment as a disciplinary tool had been abolished. This educational philosophy was especially popular in the Netherlands. Very soon after the establishment of a private Montessori school, the first public Montessori school, in Amsterdam's Corelli Street, opened its doors in 1926.

The building was part of the new Plan Zuid urban development, designed by architects of the 'Amsterdam School'. Some of their children attended our school: Friso Kramer and Onno Greiner, who were in my sister's class; Melisande Kramer, one of my friends, and Erica Kurvers, my sister's friend. Piet Kramer was to become world-famous for the beautiful cast-iron bridges he designed for Amsterdam, featuring the sculptures of Hildo Krop. Dick Greiner designed the Muzieklyceum in the Apollo Lane, which burned to the ground after the war; two new schools were built in that location. Their sons also became well-known architects.

The architecture of the Amsterdam School was largely focused on public housing works, with the aim of enhancing the working man's sense of aesthetic appreciation. The hallmark of this style was the ornamental brickwork of the homogeneous housing blocks. The band of young architects was employed by the City of Amsterdam's Public Works Department; with their interest in decorative architecture, they also had great influence on the graphic arts in Holland. It was the Dutch interpretation of art deco.

Because of my sister's friendship with Erica Kurvers, I had occasion to visit her house, as well as the architectural office of Anton Kurvers. I thought he was a very nice man. At his office I saw his graphic-design work, pamphlets and posters for the city of Amsterdam and layouts for the magazine *Wendingen*, a trailblazing journal founded by the architect Hendrik Wijdeveld, with themed issues devoted to modern architecture but also the applied arts, such as painting, dance and theatre. There, in that workroom, my interest in this new art form was born.

It was largely Amsterdam's modern, trend-setting citizenry that sent its children to the Montessori school. The children of Bert Nienhuis, a well-known potter, were also in my class. I knew from a fairly young age that I would later attend the Kunstnijverheidsschool (the art school now called the Gerrit Rietveld Academy), where these architects taught, as well as contemporary artists like Bert Nienhuis.

In 1930 came the founding of Amsterdam's Montessori Lyceum, a secondary school, and by 1934 the sixth Montessori school had opened its doors, on Nier Street. In a very short space of time Montessori education had spread like wildfire.

My father became a member of the Montessori Association, went to all the meetings and kept up with the latest developments. My mother, however, did not get involved.

That had something to do with her limited facility with the Dutch language. Her role in raising us mainly entailed making sure that we behaved properly.

When I was three I went to school for the first time. The Corelli Street school had three pre-kindergarten classrooms that prepared children for the Montessori primary school. It was a steady and easy transition, since the same learning materials were used. Mrs Van Rooy was the legendary headmistress of our preparatory school, and I was in her class. I immediately felt at home there, which was naturally the intention. There was a kitchen adapted to a toddler's size, and a 'rest nook', where you could go and read. But most of the time I was busy working. The older children were encouraged to help the youngest, and if we talked too much the teacher would write QUIET on the blackboard in big block letters, which led to the game of walking on your tiptoes and whispering.

In September – I had been at school just six weeks – a big gale blew up just as school let out. I was walking in between Frolline and my sister when a tile from the school roof landed squarely on my head. A few minutes later I was seated on the lap of a very shaken Mrs Van Rooy, whose skirt was covered in blood. This alarmed me so that my tears promptly dried up. My mother had been attending to a client, who rushed her to the school; we drove to the hospital in the client's car. There the wound was stitched up and my head bandaged. In the hospital my sister, who had been inconsolable ever since it happened, was made to sit behind a screen with Frolline. I could hear her scream and yell, 'My little sister was bonked on the head by a roof tile!'

Since I had been wearing a beret, there were no very serious consequences from this accident, although it did leave me with a dent in my head. Mrs Van Rooy, whose dress was completely ruined, came away from the incident with an haute couture gown sewn in my mother's atelier.

Until our move to Albrecht Dürer Street in 1937 we covered the distance between Willemsparkweg and Corelli Street four times a day, a twenty-minute walk.

Several times a week my father would take us to the Zuiderbad pool before dropping us at school. We had our swimming lesson while he swam laps. But we never received our swimming diplomas. One day my sister got water in her nose from jumping in; she refused to jump from then on, and since I copied her in everything she did, I wouldn't jump in either. Let the swimming instructor yell as loud as he liked, or clap his hands, we looked the other way and pretended not to hear him. In the end he just gave up on us.

The other days it was Frolline who walked us to school, and later Rika, who made the round trip on her bicycle. Rika was the one who taught us to ride our bikes because my parents, neither of whom had grown up in the Netherlands, didn't know how. Rika also taught us to skate, with the help of her fiancé, who was from Friesland. We became members of the Ice Club at the Museumplein Square, where they sprayed the ground with water as soon as the temperature dropped below freezing. Later I would skate with my friends on the Reijnier Vinkeles Quay, as well as on the Boerenwetering, a little further on. My sister stopped coming with me. It was too cold for her.

One morning on our way to school we saw little bits of burnt straw all over the streets. It was what was left of the thatched roof of the teahouse in Vondelpark. It turned out that one of my childhood haunts had gone up in flames. In summer our parents used to take us for a walk in the park every Sunday morning, and at the teahouse we would have one of those little round bottles of lemonade while my parents drank tea. A new teahouse went up in the same spot later on.

Inge, a German girl who was the other kids' favourite scapegoat, was assigned to sit next to me in class. Thanks to Frolline, I was familiar with the German language and was able to explain to her the workings of the pink tower and the brown stairs of the Montessori teaching materials. Sitting side by side, we'd unroll a little mat on the floor, on which we spelled out words in individual letters. This was one of the ways we quickly picked up the letters of the alphabet; another was to trace our fingers over sandpaper cut-outs of the letters glued onto wooden blocks. So I was able to read and write by the age of five. We learned to do sums using sticks of beads. The materials were so enticing that we loved taking them out of the cupboards. It was largely left up to us to decide what to work on that day.

Another German girl, Resi, had come to live close to us with her parents and brother in Willemsparkweg; they too had fled the persecution of Jews in Germany. She walked to school with us and was placed in my class.

Her brother Bernhard, who was fourteen, sometimes played with us too, but he came up with some rather odd games. I found it exciting, but I was also a bit scared of him. My sister once came to tell me, giggling, that he had suggested that she come and pay him a visit in the afternoon while he was taking a bath.

He asked Resi and me to steal some plums for him from the greengrocer's down the street. He himself would hide and wait for us inside his front door. I knew we were about to do something that wasn't allowed, but I was prepared to do anything he ordered us to, and I was in a state of feverish excitement. We each grabbed one plum from one of the baskets, then dashed back to him and handed him the plums through the letter box in the door. Next we were ordered to get him an apple. We failed in that assignment when the grocer stormed angrily outside and we took to our heels. The grocer complained to Rika, who told us we had better avoid Bernhard's company in future.

After we moved to Albrecht Dürer Street we didn't see him any more. I did not meet him again until the war.

Albrecht Dürer Street was a new street in a posh new neighbourhood, part of the aforementioned Plan Zuid, designed by the architect Berlage. It was built in the 1920s and 30s, and one of its most thriving streets was Beethoven Street, parallel to Albrecht Dürer Street. It was a neighbourhood largely populated by businessmen and affluent people, and rents were high. Over the course of the 1930s quite a number of German-Jewish refugees had moved in there as well: prosperous tradesmen, artists and intellectuals. German shops opened their doors, and the Café de Paris in Beethoven Street became a gathering spot for German Jews. The NO. 24 tram, leading from Central Station along Beethoven Street, was commonly known as the 'Berlin Express'.

I now lived so close to the Corelli Street school that I was allowed to walk there by myself; I just had to cross Beethoven Street. I was always very late. There was usually something I felt I had to finish at the last minute. On the way I would hear the clock on the girls' HBS secondary school on Euterpe Street start to chime, and then I'd have to race to reach the door of my school before the clock struck nine. I always hung around after school as long as possible, playing hopscotch or jumping rope with the other girls, often with Melisande Kramer, who also lived on Beethoven Street. We were usually the last ones to leave the school playground.

All the girls in my class had an autograph album. The

verses we wrote in each other's albums were usually copied from our own albums, with a minor variation here and there. We also asked our teachers to write something in our albums.

When we had a male teacher in our last year, he also wrote in my album. I read it as soon as I got it back from him. It was a little poem by Guido Gezelle:

> Ah, little beet, thou singst so sweetly,
> and thine eye, so bright to see;
> ah my beet, thou art so pretty,
> and thine eye, 'tis fixed on me;
> ah, my dear, I love thy dancing,
> thou whirlst, thou twirlst, down and up –
> quoth a little fellow, whilst gazing
> at the whirling, twirling of ...
>
> > his top!

I didn't really get it. He had added something underneath: 'Try reading this sweet little poem by the Flemish poet G. Gezelle by yourself first. Then come and find me after 4 o'clock, and we'll read it together. Your ...'

I did not go to him, I was much too shy. So I asked my father what 'top' meant. He said it was Flemish for a spinning top, but I still couldn't understand what it had to do with the rest of the poem. My father read the poem and the postscript without saying anything further, but he looked grave. He seemed angry. The next day he took us to school and stalked inside with the album under his arm. Not long afterwards we had a new female teacher.

The neighbourhood we lived in now was an attractive one. My mother, who had always felt chilly in Willemsparkweg, where every room had to be individually heated with coal stoves and electric heaters, was delighted with the central heating that made the house uniformly toasty. I now lived closer to my school friends and spent a lot of time with Inge, whose parents ran a rooming house on Händel Street, very near our house, where a number of German refugee families had taken up residence.

In our new house the pink and green salons were replicated, though on a smaller scale; but now the back parlour leading to the garden was also used as the drawing room. My sister and I had a large, sunny room upstairs where we played and did our homework. Next to our playroom was the workroom. It was quite a bit smaller than the one in Willemsparkweg. Only four girls worked there now.

On a sandy parcel of land on Clio Street just around the corner from our house in Albrecht Dürer Street, some new houses were going up; when they were built, a girl came to live on that block. I was playing ball there one day when she suddenly came up to me. 'Do you know how to throw two balls at once?' she asked. I had seen her looking at me, but I was less bold. Still, I was happy that she had made the first move.

We played outside together frequently after that, and sometimes I would go over to Bertie's house. She did not go to our school. One afternoon she took me to see her grandmother. Her older sister, who happened to be there too, announced, 'I'm going to join the *Jeugdstorm*.'* Her grandmother grew very angry and started scolding her. I knew, of course, what being in the *Jeugdstorm* meant, and didn't know what to say to Bertie, of whom I was very fond.

*Literally 'Youth Storm' and referring to Hitler Youth.

Not long afterwards, I did see her sister walking around wearing the orange and black *Jeugdstorm* cap; her little brother joined up too. Bertie told me that her mother said she didn't have to become a member if she didn't want to.

Once war broke out, her father was soon seen wearing the black Dutch Nazi uniform.

5

My father came from an Amsterdam Jewish family that consisted mainly of devout Orthodox Jews. He himself, however, belonged to the generation that considered Judaism to be a tradition rather than a religious calling. Assimilation was on the increase, and people were more and more inclined to consider themselves Jewish Netherlanders than Dutch Jews. On special occasions, however, they did honour Jewish traditions: on high religious holidays, weddings, births and funerals.

By the time my father met my mother, he had already distanced himself so thoroughly from his background that the fact that she was a Catholic didn't bother him, as long as their marriage was consecrated in the Jewish tradition. For this she would have to convert to Judaism. He was happy that she showed a sincere interest in the Jewish ways and practices taught to her by the rabbi in Paris, whom she greatly respected.

While they were living in Paris, everything was fine. My mother checked into a Jewish hospital for the birth of her first child, so that if it was a boy, everything that that involved might be taken care of according to Jewish tradition. She would not have been very happy about it, but once she gave her word she would not go back on it.

The problems started once they were back in Amsterdam. The Orthodox Jewish community would not recognise my mother as a Jew. The more liberal Paris approach did not mesh with their orthodox ideals. Amsterdam's Jewish Reform community did not exist before 1931, when it was started by Jews of German origin. But my father would not have been tempted by it in any case. By tradition he belonged to the Orthodox Jewish Community, and he wanted his wife and children to belong to it too. Neither did he want his family and his many Jewish friends to view him as an outsider.

In 1938 all his hard work finally paid off. My mother was recognised as a Jewess and now my sister and I could be registered as members of the Jewish community. For under Jewish law, we now had a Jewish mother.

6

On Sunday mornings we always went downtown with my father, first to the Cineac on Reguliersbree Street, and then to the market at Waterlooplein, where my father almost always found something that caught his eye. One day he would buy an armload of books, the next he'd sift through a pile of rusty old tools and find some obscure implement. He once drove my mother to distraction by bringing home a model of an Indian canoe, a bulky thing that for years lay on top of the bookcase at our house.

My father went to the Cineac to watch the world news. We, for our part, couldn't wait for the news to be over and the cartoons to come on: *Popeye*, *Betty Boop*, *The Little Rascals*. My father anxiously followed what was happening in Germany, but consoled himself with the thought that Germany was far away. It was unthinkable to him that the Germans might attack the Netherlands. After all, our country had remained neutral in the First World War.

In those days, a few years before the war, we often had visits from acquaintances who had escaped from Germany. I did sometimes catch a snatch here or there of their conversations, so that I was aware that whatever was happening over there in Germany was very bad, but I didn't really understand what was going on. Nobody told us, and I didn't ask. The gap between children and adults was wide. The only thing I liked to read in the newspaper was Rupert Bear, and on Sunday nights the radio was tuned to the children's programme *Ome Keesje*.

The radio was a large round Bakelite one, and my mother once told us that when they had just moved back to Amsterdam, they had at first thought they'd just try it out on approval. My mother had turned it on, and the first thing she heard was Josephine Baker singing *'J'ai deux amours, mon pays et Paris'*. My mother, who was not at all sentimental and had locked away her love for Paris deep in her heart the moment she had decided to make her life in the Netherlands, had burst into tears. The radio had been purchased outright without further ado.

In April 1940 the Germans invaded Denmark. I sculpted a little doll out of clay and set it on my cot. I made believe that it held magic powers that would stop the Germans from coming to the Netherlands.

But on 10 May – my mother had returned late the night before from France – we heard airplanes zooming about our house at night. Very early the next morning found my parents glued to the radio. Family and friends stopped by throughout the day, and there was much excited discussion and talk about escaping to England by boat. But most of those who made the attempt returned from IJmuiden defeated. Only a very small number succeeded in reaching the English coast in the handful of boats that actually managed to sail out that day.

The air raid siren went off several times a day, and then we'd have to go and sit in the cellar beneath the house until the all-clear was sounded. Everyone began stocking up on supplies and taping up the windows. My sister and I filled a shoebox with our hoard of candy, but it was all gone within a month. To me, war meant two things: that a bomb might land on our house, and that there wasn't enough food.

The paper tape on the windows did end up fulfilling its purpose some time later. The German SD* and SS divisions would move into two schools on Euterpe Street, close to where we were living in the early days of the occupation. When these schools were bombed in November of 1944 – we were long gone by then – a section of Albrecht Dürer Street was also flattened by a stray bomb. The explosion shattered the windows of our former home, but the shards were held up by the tape, and so did not fall and hurt anyone passing by. The following day we went to look. I picked up a number of twisted metal scraps, which I saved in a tin cigar box. They meant a lot to me because they came from England, bits of shrapnel from the free world.

I gradually came to understand that there was another danger facing our family if the Germans came to occupy our country, but what exactly that was, I had no idea. The Netherlands capitulated five days later, and the next day we heard that our Jewish baker, who had fled here from Germany a few years earlier, had committed suicide with his entire family. We children were kept in the dark as much as possible, but we sensed the adults' anxiety. On my way to school I tossed my little clay doll into the water of the Reijnier Vinkeles Quay canal.

Sicherheitsdienst, the intelligence service of the SS.

7

My parents knew that soon they would no longer be able to afford the steep rent of Albrecht Dürer Street. So in September of 1940 we moved to a small apartment on Hunze Street, in the Rivieren, or 'Rivers' quarter.

Like the Beethoven quarter, the Rivieren quarter was part of an urban development plan conceived by the architect Berlage. Whereas the Beethoven quarter was largely inhabited by wealthy and prominent citizens, the Rivieren neighbourhood was home to civil servants, teachers and small business owners. Both socialists and national-socialists were represented in greater numbers there than in the rest of the city.

Before the war, Jews made up a full 35 per cent of the population there. This was, amongst other reasons, because many of the German Jews seeking refuge in Amsterdam had ended up here: of the almost seven thousand Jewish immigrants officially registered in the town hall, two thousand were housed in the Rivieren quarter; a good number of outlawed German socialists and communists lived there as well.

The year 1938 had seen the opening of a new synagogue on Lek Street, very near to the house that would be my home from September 1940. The façade had (and still has) an inscription written in large Hebraic letters: 'Then I shall live among the children of Israel and never forsake them.' Oddly enough, those letters remained intact throughout the war, even though the German occupier ordered the synagogue closed for worship. I could see the synagogue from our new apartment, and also the vacant lot next door, which was used as a football field by the boys of the neighbourhood.

Before we moved to Hunze Street my parents sold many of their French antiques, as well as the paintings and the framed eighteenth-century fans, for there was no room for them in the new place. I had always loved those fans, and was sorry that we no longer had them, but later it turned out that my parents still had a large collection of fans without frames stowed away in two large boxes at the top of the wardrobe, together with some bits of antique lace. The chest of drawers that held my father's coin collection came with us in the move, but not too long afterwards it, too, disappeared.

The sale of the furnishings did not bring in much money; it was wartime and there were more pressing matters to worry about. The Indian canoe, that material reminder of our Sunday morning outings before the war, was also sold.

One advantage of the move was that it solved the problem of Bertie for me. It had been hard for me to avoid her, but I felt I could not go on seeing someone from such a notorious Dutch Nazi family. When a photo was published in the *Telegraaf* that showed Bertie, her brother and her sister sitting on a horse held by an SD officer, our friendship became completely impossible. The caption below the photo, which was taken in front of the SD headquarters on Euterpe Street, vaunted the close kinship of the people of Holland

and Germany, and the children were compared to the four Heems children of the Germanic folktale, who together rode on a magical horse.

It was a difficult time for my parents. My father's firm had gone out of business, and he now started dealing a little in old books and prints, which he had always collected and loved. The war situation also caused my mother's business to drop off sharply; a few months later it would shut down for good. The Gentile seamstresses were no longer allowed to work for her. And our maid Rika, who had been with us for years, had to be let go. My mother now took in sewing and alteration work herself, with the help of Hettie, a Jewish girl. Several actresses who had signed affidavits asserting they were not Jewish, and were therefore allowed to continue working on the stage, came to her for their wardrobe alterations. My mother did not judge them: after all, they had families, and had to put bread on the table. As the war went on, her posh former clients also came knocking again; they needed their clothes altered. My mother also passed along some sewing work to her sister-in-law Martha, who was living in poverty. Her husband, a diamond cutter, had lost his job.

My mother did not spend much time on housekeeping; she wasn't used to doing housework, and the fact that she no longer had servants to take care of it was clear from the messy rooms and kitchen we now lived in. But we still drank our tea from Sèvres porcelain cups.

When the German occupation of the Netherlands began, everything seemed much the way it was before, at least to us children.

In April 1941, Deetje came over one day to pick me up; she asked me to accompany her to her aunt's house. I knew her aunt, her father's sister: she used to come to my

Aunt Martha's house with her daughter and son David to celebrate the annual Passover Seder with us. David was a few years older than us. His father had passed away, and since his death David had taken on the role of head of the household. He was a great support to his mother. He was planning to go to Palestine, and was studying to be a teacher. We liked him very much; he was always good for a laugh. He visited us from time to time, and my mother would offer him tea in a crystal beaker in a lovely silver holder which she kept separate from our other dishes just for him: David kept kosher.

I knew that David had been gone for some time. He had been picked up in a round-up a few months earlier in Waterloo Square. His mother had received a note from him saying he was on his way to Germany to work, but since then she had heard nothing more from him. I don't know if Deetje knew what was awaiting us at her aunt's house, or if that was the reason she asked me to come along. I never asked her.

Upon entering I saw a letter lying on the table; I spotted David's name, and the words 'deceased' and 'Mauthausen'. David's mother was prone on the sofa, sobbing and wailing. I remember that Deetje went to fetch her a glass of water from the kitchen. I myself stood rooted to the spot, staring at David's mother. Never have I forgotten that picture of grief.

At the time I thought this was just an isolated case, but soon it became clear that the persecution of the Jews in the Netherlands had begun, and that David's fate had been sealed by the following incident.

Some German refugees had opened their own businesses in Amsterdam in the 1930s. Within a few years Beethoven Street had become home to, amongst other things, a fruit and vegetable stand, a photographer's studio, a greengrocer's, a butcher's, a barber and an off-licence.

In the thirties two men named Kahn and Cohen had opened an ice cream parlour called Koco, which soon became very popular, on Rijn Street in the Rivieren quarter, very close to our house, and another one on Van Wou Street, which is the continuation of Rijn Street. Kahn and Cohen were incensed about all the violence aimed at Jewish businesses in the war, and decided to form a vigilante group to protect their interests.

An incident at one of their ice cream parlours, followed by a series of escalating confrontations, was to set off the famous strike of 25 February 1941, when the population of Amsterdam rose in mass protest against the Germans' treatment of the Jews.

The Germans had found out that a gang of vigilantes made up of Jews and Gentiles had its headquarters in the ice cream parlour on Van Wou Street, a 'hornets' nest of resistance'. February 17 had been a day of unrest: over two thousand uniformed Dutch Nazis had marched through the city for the funeral of fellow member, Hendrik Koot, who had been shot by the Resistance. Fistfights broke out all along the funeral procession route, including Van Wou Street. A few days earlier, the windows of Koco's Rijn Street branch had been smashed in, and the vigilantes were ready in case the Nazis tried to wreck this one too.

The next day the two proprietors left a bottle of ammonia gas in their Van Wou Street shop and twisted open the valve. Then they took to their heels and joined the other members of their group, who had gathered at a neighbour's. When the Germans kicked in Koco's door the ammonia hit them in the face, and, stumbling backwards, they immediately started shooting. The vigilantes were soon tracked down. They were arrested the same night and horribly mistreated.

The Germans rounded up close to four hundred young

Jews in the vicinity of Waterloo Square, the heart of the Jewish quarter, in reprisal. These were transported to Mauthausen, a concentration camp located near a stone quarry. The quarry was quite notorious. Practically no one who was sent to work there survived for very long. They all died within a few months.

One of the young men picked up in the *razzia* was David.

This incident took place during my last year at the Montessori school. Towards the end of that school year I was notified that I would be placed in the Girls' Lyceum on the Reijnier Vinkeles Quay, and that I was not required to take an entrance exam. The date of that school's book fair was also announced, at which we'd be able to purchase the senior girls' books from them at half price.

In June I eagerly rode my bicycle to the new school. For years, on our walks along the Reijnier Vinkeles Quay, we had passed by the front of the Lyceum; this time, however, as a prospective student, I went in through the back gate. I parked my bicycle in the rack, having arranged to meet my father at the gate. He was taking his time getting there, and I saw Adrie, my friend from the Montessori school, coming out of the building with her mother, carrying a stack of books. I could have wept. Finally I spotted my father coming; but once inside we found that the book fair was almost over. All we were able to make off with was one well-thumbed little volume that cost 25 cents.

I was greatly impressed by the great hall with its lovely murals of prehistoric animals, and I couldn't wait for the new school year to start.

What I did not know was that my father, who had already heard the rumours that harsher measures against the Jews were on the way, had come late on purpose.

The Jews had been ordered to register with the authorities in February of 1941. Those who had just two Jewish grandparents were also ordered to register, but were for the time being still exempted from the anti-Jewish decrees that the Germans had issued at the start of the occupation. Unless they were members of a Jewish congregation.

To the Germans charged with executing the race laws, my mother was not Jewish: she had four 'Aryan' grandparents. The Nazis did, however, classify my sister and me as Jewish, and the terrible consequences of that label were soon to become clear.

8

Shortly before the start of the summer holidays, the Jewish kids were called to the headmaster's office at our Montessori school, and the senior-class children were told that the schools in which they were enrolled were no longer allowed to accept Jewish students. After school, as I and two other girls who'd been told the same thing were standing around trying to figure out what this meant, some boys sneaked up behind us chanting softly, 'Ju-huws, Ju-huws.' We were frightened, and scurried away. It was the first time that I had ever been personally confronted with anti-Semitism.

Not long after this, I found out that I wasn't allowed in the public swimming pool any more either. One morning, lined up with the other kids in my swimming club around the pool, I heard the coach announce that Jewish kids would no longer be admitted. Another girl and I turned and walked away, mortified.

A feeling of loneliness and a sense of alienation descended on me.

In the summer holidays Adrie and I still went out riding around Amsterdam several times together. But in September, once the Girls' Lyceum's new term began, I didn't see her any longer. Besides, a short while later came a new decree: Jews were no longer allowed in the homes of non-Jews. For six years Adrie and I had spent every Wednesday afternoon playing together. The Germans had successfully separated Jewish children from their Gentile counterparts.

In Amsterdam there already existed several Jewish schools for the children of religious Jews; these had been set up before the war by the Orthodox congregations. But the Jewish Lyceum was a public school, set up on orders of the occupying army and meant for Jewish students who, like me, were enrolled in the state schools. Within a few weeks, twenty-five new Jewish schools were established overall: primary schools, middle schools, and various kinds of grammar and technical schools.

The Jewish Lyceum, the school I was to attend, would not open its doors until October. The Jewish professors who were to teach us had been told that as of November 1940 they would be relieved of their state-school positions, and some months later this demotion was changed to official dismissal. In the interim the maths professor who had been fired from the Vossius Gymnasium was to teach maths to both the Jewish students of his own former school and those of the Girls' Lyceum. There was also a little group of first-year students. We met twice a week at the home of Mr Roodenburg on Stadionweg, and so I already got to know some of my future classmates.

The Jewish Lyceum was to be located in an empty school building on Stadstimmertuinen, a narrow alley between the Amstel River and Weesper Street, in an area where many Jews lived. I received a notice to attend the new school to meet my teachers and to pick up a timetable and reading list. I had never been in that neighbourhood, and my father took me there on the NO. 8 tram, which in those days was

1. Eline, around 1910

2. Eline in the middle, surrounded by her colleagues

3. Eline and Hijman, in the 1920s

4. Yvette and Eline, around 1915

5. Family Van Maarsen, 1932

6. House on Willemsparkweg: third from right

7. Jacqueline and Christiane in Vondelpark

Herinnering
aan myn
schooltyd

8. Jacqueline and Christiane in the garden of
the Montessori school, 1934

9. Class photo, Montessori school, Inge front row right, Jacqueline sitting at the other side of the 'loose letters'

10. Jacqueline, 1937–38 school year

11. Euterpe Street, at the corner of Albrecht Dürer Street,
after the 1944 bombardment

12. Razzia at Waterlooplein, 1941

Jacqueline v. Maarsen wordt uitgeno-
digd opZondag. 1. Maart bij Anne
Frank, Merwedeplein 37, te 11 uur,
voor een filmvoorstelling.

&&&& ___ &&&& ___ &&&& ___ &&&& ___

MRT 1942

Z.O.Z.

Zonder deze kaart geen toegang.

————————————

Wanneer men verhinderd is te komen,
gelieve tijdig te waarschuwen.

tel. 90441

MRT 1942

rij II plaats 2

13. Invitation to a film screening at Anne's house

14. Anne on the flat roof of the house on Merwedeplein Square in 1940. In the background, the open window that Anne and Jacqueline would use to climb outside

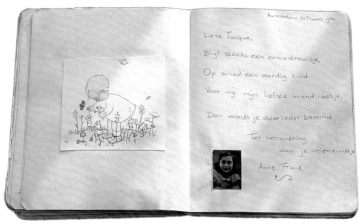

15. Anne Frank's inscription and photograph in Jacqueline's friendship album

16. Back side of Anne's New Year's card to Jacqueline

17. Left to right: Christiane, Betsy, Meta (sitting on swing), Deetje and Jacqueline, 1940

18. Jacqueline van Maarsen in 1944

19. Grietje and Jacqueline, 1947

20. Wedding of Siphra and Alex. Bridesmaids: front row left
Betsy, front row right Meta, back row left Alex's sister,
back row right Chrisje

21. Ina, Jacqueline, and Cox in the Liberator

met jullie allemaal? Ik vind het zo jammer dat i
nooit antwoord krijg. Gisteren heb ik aan Emm
iets over mevrouw geschreven, en toen kwam
ze er aan, flap, boek dicht. Hé Anne, mag ik n
eens kijken?
Nee mevrouw. Alleen de laaste blz. maar? Ne
ook niet mevrouw. Ik schrok me natuurlijk e
hoedje want daar stond zij juist als mind
aangeraam gedeponeerd. Ik heb Joop ter Heu
zo gauw uitgelezen dat ik voor Zaterdag geen
nieuwe boeken meer krijg, Als ik de laatste twe
dan ook uit heb vraag ik aan Kleiman, of ik „k
de Jongen" door Theo Thijssen, niet kan krijgen
ken jij dat? Ik wou maar dat je onze behui
hier eens kwam bekijken, hoewel het heat moe valt
lach je dood. Net is mijn vulpen? ik bedoel
moeders vulpen) leeg gegaan en met potlood
schrijf ik niet graag, dus een embrasse (sentim
teel hé, dat houd ik van Jobbje — schat over) van
Annek

Dit is de beloofde vaar-wel brie

Lieve Jacqueline,
                                                    25 - Sept.
Ik schrijf je deze brief om afscheid van je te ne
dat zal je denkelijk wel verwonderen, maar het
lot heeft het nu een maal niet anders bestemd, ik
weg (zoals je intussen natuurlijk allang gehoo
hebt) met mijn familie, de reden zal je zelf wel
Toen je me Zondagmiddag opbelde kon ik je n
zeggen, want dat mocht niet van moeder, het
huis stond toen al op zijn kop, en de huisdeur
afgesloten. Hello zou komen, maar er werd niet

22. Farewell letters from Anne to Jacqueline

ngeslaan. Ik kan niet aan iedereen schrijven
aarom di̶t̶ ᵂᵉ ik het ook alleen maar aan jou. Ik
n aan dat je niemand over deze brief spreekt
an wie je hem gekregen hebt, ook niet. Als je zo
ndelijk wilt zijn met mij geheime corresponden-
an te houden zou ik je daar zeer dankbaar
zijn. Inlichtingen mevrouw Gies!!!! Ik hoop
wij elkaar spoedig ᵂᵉᵉʳ zullen zien, maar het zal
moedelijk toch niet vóór het einde van de
og zijn. Als Lies of iemand anders je ooit vraagt
e nooit iets van mij hoort zeg dan nooit jawel,
t je brengt mevrouw Gies en ons in levensge-
r, en ik hoop ook dat je zo verstandig bent.
ᵃᵍ later natuurlijk wel vertellen, dat je eéⁿ
f van mij gehad hebt, ten afscheid. Welnu Jackie
ga je goed, ik hoop dat ik gauw een levens-
en van je ontvang en tot spoedig weerziens.
beste" ᵛʳᶦᵉⁿᵈᶦⁿ ᴬⁿⁿᵉ.
. Ik hoop dat ᵂᵉ je tot dat we elkaar terugzien
ʳ ᵃˡ̶tijd „beste" vriendinnen blijven. dáág.
        Tweede brief.   25 Sept. 1942.
ᵛᵉ Jackie,
brief heeft me erg verheugd, als er nog nie-
and van de Duitsers in onze woning geweest
kan je wel naar mijnheer Goldschmith gaan
wat boeken en schriften en spelletjes van
ns weghalen je mag ze houden of voor me
ᵂᵃ ren, maar je kunt ze ook naar mevrouw
s brengen. Ik heb je in mijn vorige brief vergeten
zeggen, dat je deze brieven niet mag bewaren,
nt niemand mag ze vinden. Snipper ze dus in

23. Jacqueline and Otto Frank, 1970

24. Eline and Hijman in Garmisch-Partenkirchen

25. Hijman, around 1920

known in Jewish circles as the 'Jerusalem Express', and which connected the Jewish quarter around Weesper Street with the Rivieren quarter. The same tramline was to be used some time later for the deportation of Jews. Since the war, there has never been another NO. 8 tram in service in Amsterdam.

Hesitantly, I entered the building, climbed a set of stairs and read on a notice board that I had been placed in CLASS 1 L2. I immediately noticed a big difference between this school and the Girls' Lyceum. Here there was no great hall with magnificent murals; instead, in front of me, just another staircase leading up to the next floor, and to my right a long corridor lined with doors. There was a sign on one of those doors reading 1 L2, and I stepped into a classroom already filled with boys and girls seated at their desks. It wasn't long before we were all chatting away, asking each other about our former schools. We seemed to have forgotten the fact that we were at this school under duress.

Moving up to secondary school was a landmark event for me, and I did my very best to shut out anything unpleasant. I was provided with a pile of new books, which I was told to wrap in paper covers and provide with labels, and when the new term began a week later I was already quite resigned to the new circumstances.

9

After my first full day at the Jewish Lyceum I cycled back home along the Amstel dyke, all abuzz with the new things I had experienced that day. New teachers, new subjects, the traditional teaching approach (as opposed to the Montessori method), which I was encountering for the first time. For maths we did not have Roodenburg; he taught the older kids. Mr Keesing, the new maths instructor, was supposed to give us our first lesson in algebra, but all he did was write $a + b = c$ on the blackboard and tell us that in his class we could completely forget about primary school arithmetic. I was very happy about that. Then he dictated some poems to us. The only time we would have to leave our classroom was for gym; for all other classes the teachers took turns coming into our classroom. I knew two of the other students: a girl from my previous school and the son of some people my parents knew. During recess I had joined their little group, and had listened rather than participated in the conversation.

Suddenly I heard someone call my name. I looked round. A short, skinny girl with shiny black hair and rather sharp features drew up beside me, out of breath.

'Are you going that way also?' she asked, pointing at the

Berlage Bridge. When I nodded yes, she declared, 'Then the two of us will ride home together from now on. I live on Merwedeplein Square.'

By the time we turned into Amstel Lane, she had already informed me that we were in the same class, that she had noticed me, that she had been meaning to speak to me after class, but that I had suddenly disappeared.

Baffled at this breathless outpouring, I braked. She did the same, and we both squealed to a stop, our feet resting next to the pedals. I hadn't noticed her in class, and felt a little awkward to have to ask her for her name.

'My name is Anne,' she said, 'Anne Frank.' I noted that her hazel eyes had dark specks in them.

We rode on together. When we arrived at the square with the landmark 'Skyscraper' building, I jumped off my bike. 'I have to go left here,' I said, 'I live on Hunze Street.' But Anne hadn't finished talking, and had me come home with her. There she introduced me to her mother as her new friend from school.

'And this is Moortje,' she said, as her black cat came meowing up to her, stalking around her and rubbing its head up against her legs. When she had fed Moortje, she took me into a small room off to the side and introduced me to her grandmother, who was seated in a comfortable chair by the window. Anne gave her a kiss and tucked the blanket more firmly around her knees. Anne did not know yet that her grandmother was terminally ill.

It turned out that Anne had been a student at the sixth Montessori school on Niers Street. I said I thought that being taught in the traditional way was easier than the Montessori method because everything was all laid out for you, but she was sorry that we weren't allowed to talk in class. That did not surprise me one bit, in light of her non-stop chatter. She told me everything there was to know about her girlfriends and her former school, and wanted to know everything about me in turn. I didn't have very much to tell, and gave her a very brief rundown. I did not have any friends in my new neighbourhood, and my friends from my old Montessori school had all gone either to the Girls' Lyceum or to a hurriedly established private Jewish Montessori school. I knew only one girl from my old school who had made the same transition as me and was now in my class, Rivka. Anne had already formed an opinion about her: untrustworthy and stuck-up.

At Anne's I felt at home right away. I liked her spunkiness and the way she had initiated our friendship. Her mother did not say very much. She spoke with a strong German accent. Anne told me later that she had tried to learn Dutch by taking lessons, but had soon given up. Her mother missed her former life in Germany; she missed her family and friends. They had moved from Frankfurt to the Netherlands in 1933, and she was having a hard time adapting.

I was immediately struck by the difference between Anne and her older sister Margot, who came home a little later. She wasn't as outgoing as Anne, mature for her age and rather introverted. Anne immediately started telling enthusiastic stories about her first day at school and announced, putting her hand on my arm, 'And *this* is my new friend.' Margot amiably asked my name, and when Anne asked her what she thought of the new school, she answered coolly, 'Oh, it's fine.' Then she left the room to start her homework. Anne told me Margot had been at the Girls' Lyceum for the past three years, and was now in the fourth form of the Jewish Lyceum, together with her friend Jetteke.

Anne showed me her movie-star collection and then said

we should do our homework together. I phoned home to tell them where I was. 'Say that you're staying for dinner,' Anne cried.

So it was that on that first day I also met her father. He took the time to have a long conversation with me; I told him that I was enrolled in the Jewish school instead of the Girls' Lyceum despite the fact that my mother was not classified as Jewish by the Nazis. He looked at me gravely and said, 'I think I ought to have a word about that with your parents.' In light of what my mother was to do later, I assume that he kept his word.

As I was leaving, Anne announced that tomorrow she would go home with me to meet my parents and sister.

I wasn't sure how I felt about that. These days I wasn't too keen on having friends over. I wasn't quite sure when this had begun, but my parents' relationship had markedly deteriorated. The relative luxury they had enjoyed before the war had given way to a day-to-day struggle to keep their heads above water, which did not do much for the atmosphere at home. Added to that, my mother berated my father for landing our family into trouble because he'd been so set on registering us as members of the Jewish community. Ignoring her warnings, he had refused to see the writing on the wall even as late as 1938, optimist that he was.

Anne paid no attention to my reluctance, however, and the next day we did our homework at my house.

From that day on we were inseparable. We rode home together the way Anne had proposed on the first day. We did our homework together – Anne was far more conscientious about this than I was; I helped her with maths, which wasn't her strong suit.

After a few days, Anne firmly declared that I was her best

friend and she mine. I agreed, although I could not have foreseen the consequences.

My parents and Anne's got along well.

That wasn't necessarily a given. In general, Dutch Jews and German Jews moved in separate circles. The German Jews who had had the means to move to the Netherlands were for the most part wealthy. They considered their Dutch counterparts not very highly cultured and of a lower class. They had settled in the best sections of Amsterdam, which led to envy on the part of the Dutch Jews, who further considered the immigrants too noisy. They were worried that by drawing attention to themselves the German Jews would stir up latent anti-Semitism in Holland.

Our parents became acquainted through Anne and me. Thanks to their shared background in Frankfurt, where my father had spent the greater part of his youth, he and Otto Frank soon became fast friends. Mr Frank often came to our home. He spoke fluent French and he and my mother would have long conversations in that language.

My mother had undergone a kind of metamorphosis. She now went around in an old dressing gown most of the time. She wasn't the type to judge people by the clothes they wore, and she didn't have a snobbish bone in her body. She'd had the admiration and respect of both our maids and the baronesses she had counted amongst her clients. She was very busy these days. Not only did she have her sewing to do, she now also had to take care of the house. My sister helped her with the shopping and cooking, for she was no longer going to school. The Jewish high school was not for her; what she had studied at the Montessori school did not mesh with the traditional secondary school curriculum. After a while she found a job working in a bookshop.

I paid little attention to any of this. I was busy with my homework and my friends, and I wasn't home most of the day. Domestic matters didn't interest me. I considered it quite natural that my mother confided more in my sister than in me; after all, she was the eldest and they spoke French together. My mother and I, on the other hand, had a rather eccentric way of communicating. She spoke to me in French, I answered her in Dutch, or the other way round. To outsiders witnessing this, it must have seemed pretty strange. The fact that my mother had never made much of an effort to learn Dutch now proved a handicap. In the shops people took her for a German, which irked her no end.

Anne wrote in her diary, 'Recently I met Jacqueline van Maarsen at the Jewish Lyceum. We hang out together all the time and she's my best friend now.'

It wasn't always easy being Anne's best friend. She was very demanding and quickly jealous. And our personalities were quite opposite. Yet we were kindred souls. We discussed everything together, and copied each other in everything we did. I imitated the way she held her pen, between the index and middle finger, and it did improve my handwriting somewhat. She would sometimes write in block letters, a habit she had taken over from me.

We read the same books. The series about the spunky teenager Joop ter Heul, by Cissy van Marxveldt, was our favourite. Not only were the adventures of the books' spirited gang of heroines vividly drawn; we also liked to compare ourselves to those girls, who lived in such a free and untroubled world. We never tired of reading scene after scene aloud to each other. We would act out the marriage proposal scene in book II, *The problems of Joop ter Heul*, taking turns playing Joop or Leo van Dil. We'd burst out laughing every time Leo made an ardent attempt to kiss Joop, only to be fobbed off with a cherry bonbon or a *marron glacé*.

The ping pong club we started that year was in every way based on the one called the 'Jopopinoloukicoclub' in the Joop ter Heul series. We'd gather at the house of Ilse, a girl in our class. Her mother let us use the dining table in the living room as our ping pong table, and we stretched a net across it. We weren't exactly fanatic about it: there was always a good deal more gossip and laughter than ping pong going on.

The school was an important part of our lives. We loved our classes and the unique atmosphere of the Jewish Lyceum. Teachers and students were all in the same boat, and that formed a bond between us. We were a close-knit group. In those early days the menace outside didn't seem to filter into the school. Most of the professors had come from Amsterdam's top secondary schools, for example, the two gymnasiums and the Girls' Lyceum. We had quite a few hours of German at school, as decreed by the occupation; we had to learn the German script and read Gothic typeface. English was held over until the second form. In that respect, our school was in the same boat as the other state schools. In the first form we also had to learn French. I was pretty bad at it, at least when it came to memorising the grammar. Learning by heart was something we had hardly ever done at the Montessori school, and I considered it a waste of time, because I thought I knew it all anyway. When the teacher realised that I basically never did my homework, he got very annoyed. He started piling on extra homework for me, a form of punishment I had never had at my previous school and which may have been the only thing to which I really applied myself. Mr Keesing, the maths teacher, taught us algebra and geometry, but he also gave us riddles to solve and liked to tell jokes.

This only encouraged Anne to start chatting with the kids around her, which often led her into trouble with the teacher. She sometimes forgot she was no longer at a Montessori school. She did not participate much in gym; that was because of her shoulder, which she had once dislocated. Unlike me – I didn't like to stand out in a crowd – she enjoyed occupying a unique position.

For me, drawing class was a revelation. For some reason we had not been allowed to draw freehand at the Montessori school: we drew figures by tracing circles, squares and triangles and then colouring them in. My artistic talent suddenly blossomed at the Jewish Lyceum and I always received top marks for the clay pots, tin cans and wicker baskets that I liked to draw. In Dutch class we read Nicolaas Beets and extracts from *Woutertje Pieterse*, and our Dutch teacher, Mr Pos, had us rehearse a play, something Greek, for which we wore garments made from bed sheets. 'I'd rather have some rice,' was a line from that play. I had never heard that expression and I didn't understand what it had to do with the rest of the text. Pos survived the war and eventually became the head of Amsterdam's acting academy.

I soon began to feel quite at home at this school. Being Jewish was not an important part of it, neither for me nor for the other students, most of whom had not had a religious upbringing. The subject of religion did not come up, and if any students did have Hebrew lessons, it was done after school. I wasn't aware of Anne being particularly religious either. We simply didn't talk about it. When I told her the story of David's disappearance, she was shocked, but when I told her about his dream of going to Palestine, Anne said without hesitation that her country was the Netherlands, and that she hoped to become a Dutch citizen after the war.

Hitler had stripped the Franks of their German citizenship; they were stateless.

Still, even here at school there were times when I felt excluded – the feeling of being different from the others. In history we were supposed to be studying ancient Greece and Rome, but our teacher suddenly switched over to the history of the Spanish Inquisition and about the suffering of the Jews in the fifteenth century. The way he told it, the Catholics didn't come off looking very nice, naturally. The subject was an appropriate one for the times we were living in, but I felt myself shrink at the fanatic and aggressive way he described it. My mother's Catholicism weighed on me heavily. I did not speak of it with anyone, not even Anne. The result was that I couldn't concentrate on this teacher's lessons at all, and I received a big, fat F for history on my report card.

Then my father gave me the book *Myths and Legends of Greece and Rome*. He thought it would encourage me to take an interest in history. Anne, who was especially fond of the pictures of the various gods and goddesses in that book, asked for the same book for her birthday.

When we didn't have any homework we'd play a game of Monopoly or other board games, and our sisters would often play too, or Hannah, a friend of Anne's from her primary school days, or one or two of our new classmates. As for Rivka, the friend who had come with me from our primary school, Anne had a bit of a problem with her. During that school year she was to write in her diary, 'Jacque is totally taken in by her, and that's a great pity,' but I was never conscious of being taken in by Rivka; something must have happened that I wasn't aware of.

We spent hours sorting through Anne's collection of film stars and adding to it with photos we cut out of film or women's magazines. We both collected picture postcards, and we would trade these with each another. We might even be charitable enough to donate one for free, if it was one the other particularly liked. I still have a card of Shirley Temple addressed to Margot Frank. I did not have a film-star collection. My only idols were Shirley Temple and Deanne Durbin. Before the war I had seen some Shirley Temple films, and once I went to the cinema with my sister to see a film with Deanne Durbin, *One Hundred Men and a Girl*. She had been invited by the mother of one of her friends, and I was invited to come along. Anne's collection consisted mainly of German film stars. She swooned over the pictures of these actresses with their long, blonde, wavy tresses. Most of them acted in Nazi propaganda films; I don't think she ever saw those films, they were for adults only. When the war broke out she was ten years old, and from September 1941 we were no longer allowed in the cinemas.

Anne adored nice clothes. I read her a cutting from the *Haagsche Post*, which said, among other things: 'One of the most striking figures at the Christmas dinner was Mrs van H. B. of Aerdenhout, who appeared in a gorgeous gown of gold lace, which beautifully set off her strawberry-blonde hair.' It was accompanied by a note Mrs van H. B. had sent my mother: *'Ci-joint je vous envoie, parce que je trouve que c'est si amusant, l'article dans le* Haagsche Post *sur la robe que vous avez faite.'** My mother told me the rest of the story. The two of them had chosen the fabric for the gown together, but my mother, who had seen the fabric at night, by artificial light, had ordered a different colour gold against the client's wishes, because she had been sure that the fabric she had chosen would clash with her hair.

All the other evening gowns were also described in that

*'I enclose, because I think it's so amusing, the article in the *Haagsche Post* about the dress you made for me.'

article, and the last sentence made us swoon: 'Among the young ladies present, the dark tresses of spirited Lady van Pallandt stood out, while Miss Francken, tall, blonde and more ethereal than ever, in a cloud of soft yellow crêpe georgette, attracted the attention of all who were present.'

We dreamed about 'after the war', when we, too, would appear at balls and parties in 'clouds of crêpe georgette'. Our models were, of course, the heroines in the books of Cissy van Marxveldt.

But in the meantime we contented ourselves with the parties organised by Anne. Films were rented, and boys and girls in favour were invited over to Anne's house. So it was on the Sunday following her thirteenth birthday. I helped her with the arrangements and we typed out invitations on her father's typewriter. We took great pains over the seating arrangements, deciding who should sit next to whom, and we lined up the chairs in rows. It was supposed to look as much as possible like a real theatre.

So that Sunday afternoon after her thirteenth birthday, Anne had stars in her eyes as her classmates filed in and she eagerly opened her presents. She did always love being the centre of attention. In the days leading up to this she had told everyone she met about her birthday, not only kids but adults as well. My father brought her a bunch of sweet peas for her birthday, which she listed in her diary amongst the other gifts she received that day.

The show began with a short. We saw Miep Gies in a small kitchen making jam. Miep lived across from us on Hunze Street, and she worked for Anne's father at his office. The short was an advertisement for Opekta, a gelatin product for making jam, which Mr Frank's firm distributed. Then came the main attraction, an instalment of the Rin-Tin-Tin series. Rin-Tin-Tin was a brave dog having all sorts of adventures.

When it was over we sat and discussed it as Anne went round offering the biscuits we had baked the day before. Margot and her mother poured the lemonade. Mr Frank packed up the borrowed film projector and went to return it.

It made me think of our own pre-war parties, when my father would take out his magic lantern and show us slides. The magic lantern had disappeared in the move, and with it the happy atmosphere of our home before the war.

Anne was still in a bubbly mood when everyone had left and we were sitting around sorting her presents. The reason I remember it so well is that I didn't see the diary her parents had given her the day before. This surprised me, because it was her most significant present. But just how significant it was to become, Anne would never know.

There were more parties like these, thrown by the other kids; for public cinemas and theatres were now off-limits to Jews.

Later that year, when Anne had already disappeared, I saw a cabaret show by two Jewish performers, Johnny & Jones. Since the Germans liked to raid events that would have large numbers of Jews in attendance, my parents were very reluctant to let me go. The performance was held at the Joodse Invalide, the Jewish rest home in Weesperplein Square.

When spring came, we would often bask in the sun on the 'flats', the flat roof just outside the attic at Anne's house. At the back of the hall was a staircase leading up to the top floor. At the end of the upstairs corridor was the garret room that the Franks rented out, and outside that was a window through which we could clamber outside onto the roof. There we would tell each other all sorts of secrets.

Anne was very curious about the sexual relations between men and women, and quizzed her father about it. He came up with all kinds of evasive replies, which she would pass on to me and which I found hilarious; but I was able to enlighten her somewhat further, for my sister had given me the main gist of it some years before. Anne grumbled that her sister, who was several years older, never told her anything and treated her like a little kid.

One time Anne had found a little cardboard carton belonging to her mother, and we avidly read the slip of paper we found inside. It was the instructions leaflet for sanitary tampons. We tore it up into little snippets.

In her diary Anne may have described our classmate Rivka in the most extravagantly unpleasant terms; she was, nevertheless, the only other girl with whom we ever shared our secret engrossment with sex. At Rivka's house the three of us, red-cheeked, had sat poring over a certain book she had found in her parents' linen cupboard.

Anne did once engage the most mature boy in our class in a conversation on the subject, and managed to pry some information out of him, which she later passed on to me. We found his assertions most remarkable. We were quite well up on the theory by now, but finally we had some insight into the practice.

Then Anne found it necessary to grill the youngest boy in our class, who had been a primary school classmate of hers, on his understanding of the subject. It made her feel more grown-up, which was very important to her. At home Anne was considered the little one, sometimes a bit of a nuisance. It made her furious not to be taken seriously.

She once came to see me, fuming, after going to the dentist in Jan Luyken Street with her mother and Margot. Margot had gone shopping afterwards with her mother; Anne hadn't been allowed to come along. She was mad at her mother and jealous of Margot. I thought Margot and her mother were

always very nice and very patient with her, and I told her so.
But it didn't help. She stayed mad.

In spite of the fact that our personalities were so
different, we remained 'best friends', something Anne kept
emphasising verbally as well as in writing. When she gave
me back my friendship album after writing a little verse in
it for me, I was touched by the personal twist she had given
the otherwise well-worn rhyme. She had inserted the words
'my dearest friend'.

Amsterdam, 23 March 1942

Dear Jacque,
Be always a ray of sun
A darling schoolgirl too
Then to you my dearest friend
I'll be forever true

Remember your dear friend
Anne Frank

She had pasted a picture of herself underneath. She had
asked me several times for my picture, but unlike Anne, who
possessed a whole arsenal of pictures of herself, I wasn't able
to come up with a suitable photo that fast.

I probably just didn't think it was that important. After all,
we saw each other every day!

'This is the only letter I have from Jacqueline van Maarsen,
I did beg her over and over again for a picture of herself, and
she said she would try to find one. Now, on 28 September
1942, it's too late,' I would read in her diary years later. How
it weighed on my conscience!

Anne couldn't really accept the idea that I might sometimes
wish to spend time in the company of other girls, and she

also didn't understand that I did not share her need to have people around all the time. She just *had* to have someone to talk to or play with, or she would get dreadfully bored. I occasionally broke Anne's strict rules by arranging to meet one of my classmates, Ilse or Hannah. On 19 June 1942, Anne wrote in her diary: 'Jacque is suddenly very taken with Ilse and is being very childish and snotty to me.'

'She was just jealous,' her father said to me when he gave me Anne's original diary to read years later and noticed my bewildered expression upon reading that comment. He had never before shown me that line from Anne's diary, nor had he considered it suitable for inclusion when he prepared the first edition of *The Secret Annex*. 'I just viewed it as something written in the heat of the moment,' he added, and to prove the point he showed me the lines she had inserted later: 'Right now she's being very sweet to me again and I hope it stays that way,' and, 'I now feel quite differently about the things I wrote before but I can't tear any pages out of my diary.'

And what about the letters, too, I thought to myself, the letters she wrote to me from hiding, attesting to our very close friendship. Fortunately she copied them into her diary, otherwise they would have been lost.

On the same occasion I also asked Otto why he had changed my name to 'Jopie' in Anne's diary, and how he had come to choose that name. 'I didn't do that,' he replied, 'it was Anne herself who came up with that name for you. When she was copying her diary and getting it ready for publication, she compiled lists of name changes.'

It was only decades later that I discovered the answer to the question of how Anne had come up with those names, when I read the original version of Anne's diaries in *The Diaries of Anne Frank, The Critical Edition*, published in 1986.

That was when I discovered that Anne's diary had been inspired by the Joop ter Heul books, and that she had been writing in the same style, at least to start with. She had also adopted the letter-and-diary form from the first of the Cissy van Marxveldt series, *Joop ter Heul's Schooldays*.

When she rewrote her diaries in the secret annex, she gave me the name Jopie, after van Marxveldt's heroine, Joop, and she gave the character she was addressing in her diary the name of Joop's best friend, Kitty. I noted that in her original diary she had also written letters to the other girls in Joop ter Heul's gang; I recognised the names of the other members of the 'Jopopinoloukicoclub'.

The Institute for War Documentation's critical edition of the diaries, published in 1986, was made necessary in order to dispel the doubts that had arisen about their veracity. Over the years their authenticity had repeatedly been assailed by neo-Nazis. It was, after all, proof that the Holocaust had actually taken place. Otto Frank had already been involved in a number of lawsuits about this.

The Holocaust deniers had pounced on the confusion that had come from the fact that there were three different versions of the diary. The first version is the original diary, which Anne began on her thirteenth birthday. Some time later she decided to revise and edit it with a view to having it published when the war was over. That is the second version, which she herself dubbed *The Secret Annex*. She rearranged the text and consolidated parts that had been written at different times. She expanded certain sections, and cut other sections down. She was not yet finished with this project when she was arrested.

The third version is Otto Frank's selections from his daughter's writings. This became the first published edition, in 1947. He put together a version by joining the first part, the one that Anne had already revised, with the last, which she had not yet finished. He left out some passages which he did not consider important, or that he felt were hurtful to his late wife. The passages in which Anne writes about the changes in her body were also omitted, at the publisher's request. A number of minor corrections were further made. Anne was four when she came to Amsterdam from Germany, and she had learned to speak Dutch fluently. But at home German was frequently spoken, by her mother and also by many visitors. Therefore some Germanisms would, from time to time, creep into her work.

In *The Diaries of Anne Frank* the three versions appear side by side. The research into the handwriting, paper and ink is also documented there. A New Year's card that Anne had sent me in January 1942 and my own friendship album were both important pieces of evidence.

Anne often asked me to spend the night at her house, or else she'd invite herself to mine. She usually brought a suitcase containing everything needed for a sleepover, plus of course a toiletry bag with curlers, hairbrush and cape. She spent a great deal of time attending to her black hair, which reached down to her shoulders. She would brush it for a long time every night to give it a beautiful shine.

She decided she would come to my house for a sleepover the night before my birthday. That way she could be the first to wish me a happy birthday and the first to give me a present. I still have the book she gave me: *Hup Loek!* by Aleid Ages van Weel, subtitled *A novel for older girls*. It's about high school, swimming, hockey, horseback riding, and it ends, as does every book for girls, with the upcoming marriage of Loek, the heroine of the tale. It now has pride of place next to my old copy of *Joop ter Heul*, the *Myths of Greece and Rome*, and the Monopoly game we used to play so often. The fact that her grandmother had passed away just the previous day may possibly have had something to do with that sleepover as well.

Easter came, and Anne had a low mark on her report card for maths. The teacher had recommended tutoring for Anne; without it she would probably not be allowed to move up to the next form. Naturally her parents already knew that by the start of the new school year Anne would be in hiding. But for us children everything was supposed to continue as normally as possible. Not even nosy Anne had any inkling of the secret plans her parents were making to go into hiding.

Meanwhile, Anne's bicycle was stolen. She and I went to the police together to report the theft; in hindsight a rather pointless exercise, since just a few weeks later all Jews would have their bicycles confiscated. Anne now had to go quite a distance on foot to her tutor on Okeghem Street, and she asked me to walk with her.

This turned into a pleasant biweekly routine; walking there took almost longer than the lesson itself. I would sit in the sun on the stoop and wait for her to come out again. We'd walk back along the canal discussing some of our many common interests. The trees were already starting to turn green and we were happy in each other's company. The possibility that we might soon have to part did not really cross our minds. It was true that we had promised to write each other a farewell letter in case one of us had to go away, but we could not or would not give it any further thought. We could not even begin to imagine that this life would soon be gone for ever. The intensive deportations of Jews had not yet begun.

We did, however, talk about feeling threatened by the great number of German troops now dominating Amsterdam's urban landscape. At a certain point in the school year, it became compulsory for all Jews to wear a yellow Star of David prominently visible on their clothing. It made us immediately recognisable, and quite vulnerable. This made it easier to check if people were biding by the decrees that were being issued. Not only the German troops, but also Dutch Nazis, or just people willing to report you for a handful of guilders, posed a danger. You could be arrested for crimes like sitting on a park bench, or wandering into a shop that was 'forbidden to Jews'. The sense of menace hanging over our heads has stayed with me always. In her diary, Anne wrote, 'Jopie used to say to me, "I don't dare do *a thing* any more, because I'm always afraid it isn't allowed."'

Anne somehow managed to turn everything into a party. Never have I met anyone who enjoyed life with as much gusto as she did. I basked in the warmth of her affection, and did my very best to return the friendship in kind.

Sometimes that was hard to do: because of my own more reticent personality, I often didn't quite know what to do with her effusive declarations of friendship and ardent love. At one of our sleepovers she did something that embarrassed me quite a bit. She herself wrote about it in her diary: 'I proposed to Jacque that we should feel each other's breasts, as proof of our friendship. Jacque refused.'

She wasn't at all happy that I would not go along with her suggestion. 'We're best friends, aren't we?' she protested. I agreed, but said I didn't think it was necessary to prove it to her in this particular way. To appease her I let her give me a peck on the cheek. Her curiosity made me uncomfortable. Breasts fascinated her, she herself had been experimenting with cotton wool stuffed into one of Margot's bras, and she had just discovered that I was not in need of any such artificial means.

I made it clear to her in my own way just where I drew the line, and also that she had to allow me a little more breathing room. 'After all, you sometimes go walking with Hello, don't you?' I said, to show her that I, for my part, was prepared to give her that freedom. Hello was a boy who lived nearby, on Zuider Amstel Lane. Anne had noticed that I had been spending quite a bit of time with Ilse lately, in an attempt to extricate myself from the relentless stranglehold Anne imposed on me. She was afraid that Ilse would become my new best friend. I, however, was perfectly aware that I needn't fear any competition from Hello, because I knew how very fond Anne was of me.

This conversation cleared the air of the strain that had arisen between us for a few days.

That spring we often went to an ice cream shop not far from where we lived, Oase, which was for Jews only. It was a place where Jewish youngsters met and hung out. We bought our ice cream cones and huddled in little groups on the pavement outside, chatting. Anne would sometimes break away from our little group of girls to speak to a boy she knew. She was cheerful and vivacious and the boys must have thought she was cute. She liked to think that they fancied her. We didn't notice much of that going on, actually. She did walk up and down the street once or twice holding hands with Hello, constantly glancing over her shoulder to make sure that we saw it. Hannah, Ilse and I teased her about Hello, in whose eyes we were just a bunch of little kids. Hello, who was already sixteen, and who would survive the war, later said that he always found Anne quite cute and smart, but that the one who had really caught his eye was the unattainable Margot; he thought she was sweet and pretty.

And I knew perfectly well that Anne was just flirting a bit, that she wanted to show off to us that a boy of sixteen was interested in her. She was so keen to experience everything. From the day that she went into hiding, Hello's name was never again mentioned in her diary.

On 30 June 1942, Anne writes: 'Saturday night Jopie slept at my house, but Sunday afternoon she was at Hannah's and I was bored to death.'

When I read that in Anne's diary, I was struck by the lack of jealousy in that remark, because the afternoon in question had left me with a guilty feeling towards my best friend which I never had the chance to get off my chest; a week later she was gone. For that reason I have never forgotten that afternoon. Hannah and I sat next to each other on her bed and Hannah complained that Anne was being mean to her again. I listened to her story and sympathised with her. I didn't think Anne was being very nice to Hannah either.

Since I visited Anne's family so often, it struck me one day that all the chairs in the room were gone, replaced by a different set of dining chairs. When I expressed my surprise, I was told that they had gone to be re-upholstered, a hastily invented excuse. I had come very close to discovering their secret. But I didn't suspect a thing, and thought to myself, naïvely: Don't they have anything more serious to worry about than some chairs that may be starting to look a bit worn? In my opinion they were still perfectly fine.

On Monday, 6 July, Hannah came round to tell me that the Frank family was gone. 'They have gone to Switzerland!' she added excitedly. Her parents had heard it from the Franks' lodger. He had found a note clearly intimating that that was their destination. Anne and I had spent some time on the phone together the night before, but there had been no hint that she would be gone by the next day.

I was happy for Anne and her family that they'd managed to leave in time, and that feeling prevailed over the empty feeling I suddenly had because my best friend had disappeared. Still, I expected to see her again soon enough, because I was convinced that the war could not last very much longer.

Hannah and I wondered if Anne had left her diary behind at her house on Merwedeplein Square. She was always so tight-lipped about it, and had confided to me that it contained descriptions of every boy and girl in our class. We decided to go up to Merwedeplein to see if we could find the diary. We were just dying to find out what she had written about us. We were able to get in because Mr Goldschmith, who sublet a room from them, was home.

The beds had not been made and the kitchen had not been cleaned up. That was a most unusual state of affairs for this family. One memory of our venture to the Franks' abandoned home has never left me: it's the sight of Anne's unmade bed, and next to it Anne's new shoes, lying there as if she had just kicked them off. Anne had been so taken with these shoes, and so proud of the soles, which were made of laminated wood lined with rubber: our wooden shoes (leather being almost completely unavailable in those days) normally had rigid soles. I could not understand why she hadn't taken them with her, but later it did occur to me that in Switzerland, of course, she'd be able to buy shoes made of real leather.

I peeked into the kitchen. Where was Moortje? I asked Mr Goldschmith. 'Moortje is at the neighbour's,' he said. What a heart-wrenching goodbye that must have been. Anne was so crazy about that cat.

What I did not tell Hannah was that I had also been hoping to find the promised letter of farewell, and I poked around a little longer to see if Anne had left it for me anywhere. I didn't see it, and I did not want to enquire about it. It would be three years before I received that letter. It said, amongst other things: 'If the Germans haven't yet been in our house, you could go to Mr Goldschmith and pick up some of our books and board games. You can keep them for yourself, or save them for me; or else you could give them to Mrs Gies.'

It turned out that, besides her diary and her film-star and postcard collections, she had left behind all her board games and books. I did see her *Variété* game lying around, a recent birthday present, which we had played furiously for several weeks. I was almost tempted to take it, but I didn't. The Germans had declared it was forbidden to remove anything from a home abandoned by its owners, and so we left everything just the way we found it.

Not long after Anne went into hiding, other kids at our school began to stay away as well. The *razzias* had begun in the Jewish quarter and you were never sure who was 'hiding' and who had been 'taken'. These two words suddenly acquired utterly new meanings. The young boy whom Anne had so kindly briefed about the birds and the bees was one of the first to drop out of school. Many years later I met him again: he had spent the war in hiding. What he told me when I saw him again was that he had been very embarrassed by Anne's 'sexual instruction', and that the memory of it had bothered him for quite a while afterwards.

The majority of the children at our school, however, were

deported to the concentration camps. Most of them never returned. Like Ilse. She was gassed at Sobibor on 2 April 1943. On that same day in 1942, she'd written something in my friendship album about 'a long and happy life'. How ignorant we children were then of the very real perils ahead!

Teachers, too, stopped coming to school. After the war I heard what had happened to a number of them, either through their own writings, or through the recollections of others.

Gerard Reve, in his book *Nader tot U* (Nearer to Thou), tells of the death of Dr Biegel, the biology teacher. She committed suicide upon receiving her summons for Camp Westerbork. She had been Reve's teacher at the Vossius Gymnasium, until she had been made to resign from that school by the Germans.

I met some of the teachers again after the war. The French teacher we had had at the Jewish Lyceum came to teach at the Girls' Lyceum after the war. We were done with French grammar by then, and I always earned top marks for the prose translations we were now given to do. But his attitude to me had not improved. He could not keep order in class, and whenever there was any sort of trouble, I was the one who was punished, even if I'd had nothing to do with it. I had the feeling he resented the fact that I was still alive. I was glad when he resigned the following year.

As the number of students and teachers dwindled, the classes were combined. Jacques Presser became our history teacher. His wife had been arrested with forged papers on a train on her way to meet up with her parents, who had found a hiding place somewhere in the countryside. The day after her disappearance Presser read aloud in class the story of Dante and Beatrice's meeting in paradise. Overcome with emotion, he ran out of the classroom sobbing, leaving behind a roomful of stricken students sitting in total silence. For a long time after the war he went on hoping against hope that his wife would return. Even after he had seen her name on the list 'Gassed at Sobibor', he continued to hope for a miracle. He would later become a professor at the University of Amsterdam and write a classic work about the persecution of the Jews, *Ashes in the Wind*.

After Anne's disappearance I went back to seeing more of Rivka. She and her parents had come to the Netherlands in 1930, fleeing the pogroms in Poland. Rivka once told me that they'd taken nothing with them except for some diapers for the baby. Her father soon had a thriving clothing business in Amsterdam. I often went to her house; she lived in the Willemsparkweg neighbourhood. Her parents often fought, yelling at each other in Polish. It didn't seem to bother Rivka very much.

She had grown into a pretty girl. She had lovely black corkscrew curls. The ringlets that Anne had tried so hard to fashion using pin curls, were natural in Rivka's case. There were always boys swarming around her, and bands of them would come and visit her at home. On such occasions she would ask me to come over, as well as Nannie, a girl in our class who lived nearby. Nannie and Anne couldn't stand each other, so I had never had any contact with Nannie until now.

Rivka disappeared a few months after Anne. Into hiding, it later turned out.

10

By the time that the transportation of Jews living in Holland via the concentration camp Westerbork to Germany and Poland was in full swing, towards the end of 1942, it was becoming increasingly clear that the Germans had initiated a program of out-and-out genocide, the so-called *Endlösung der Judenfrage*, Final Solution. In order to achieve a 'total extermination of the Jewish race,' Jews from all the German-occupied countries of Europe were deported to concentration camps. The reason initially cited, 'sent to work in Germany' became quite implausible when old people, children and pregnant women were ordered to report for deportation. The camps became ever more crowded as the organisation became more efficient. Hard labour, torture and starvation turned out to be too slow for the Germans as an extermination method. The first rumours of gassing and subsequent incineration to erase all evidence of it soon started making the rounds. Many people could not and would not believe it, my father among them.

But my mother refused to let herself be lulled to sleep by the hopeful optimism. She believed the unbelievable. Her German cousin by marriage, Else, had told her about it. The husband of Else's sister was with the SD on Euterpe

Street, and he knew what had been decided at the Wannsee Conference: the annihilation of the Jews.

Her brother-in-law's friend, who was an SD member, but also a fervent anti-Nazi, would frequently go to Else's home for meetings with a Dutch Resistance cell. They were betrayed. One night their street was blocked off at both ends, and everyone was arrested, including Else and her Jewish husband, who was my father's cousin. The German Resistance agent was hung a few days later, while the Dutch Resistance fighters were incarcerated. Else and her husband were sent to separate concentration camps, Else to the Vught concentration camp; she was released six months later. Her husband was put on a train to Westerbork, to await deportation to the extermination camp, where he died.

My mother realised that it would soon be a matter of life or death for her children, and she resolved to do what she had to do. She decided to have my father's 1938 bid to register us as Jewish children annulled. When she first started with this, my father, had he known about it, would have strongly objected, so she warned us not to breathe a word about it.

I had blind faith in my mother. I knew that everything would turn out all right for us if she took charge.

One fine day she set out from home in full regalia; smartly dressed in an outfit she had thriftily preserved, topped off with an elegant hat. A little greyer, a little thinner perhaps, but thanks to some well-applied make-up she was every bit the *Française* she had been before the war. She was confident that she would be able to accomplish her mission. She raised quite a few eyebrows in the tram on her way to Euterpe Street (now called Gerrit van der Veen Street); after two years of war, most people were looking a little down-at-heel. At the Euterpe Street HQ she registered with the duty officer and informed him she wished to speak to a senior SD commander who could speak French. She had started by addressing the duty officer in French, but when she saw that he did not understand her, she switched to the German she had picked up from needing to communicate with Mathilde and Frolline.

Flustered by her confident attitude, the officer had her shown up to the SD higher command. Just as was customary in pre-war Holland, the German middle and upper classes spoke French; French culture was greatly admired in Germany. The officer who received her spoke fluent French. She came to the point immediately.

'You have to help me,' she said. 'My husband is a Jew, and he had me registered as a Jewess without my consent, and now my two children are in danger.'

The man was impressed by her looks and her personality. He was favourably disposed towards a woman who showed such disloyalty to her Jewish husband by portraying him in this way.

Her ruse worked. She was given an assurance that if she could submit the birth and baptism certificates of her own four grandparents, our registration in the Jewish congregation would be annulled, as would our classification as Jews in the German rolls.

My mother immediately set to work. It turned out, however, that obtaining the necessary papers wasn't easy if you needed them in a hurry. Germany had not yet invaded the region in France where my grandparents had been born, and this slowed things down considerably. Time was of the essence. My sister was almost sixteen years old, and that meant that she, like her peers, would receive a summons any day now to report for 'work camp'.

Uncle Albert came to the rescue. He was aware of the difficulties his sister was facing, and appealed to an uncle who was married to my grandfather's sister. That uncle was the manager of a famous restaurant on Paris's Champs Elysées. His establishment was a favourite haunt of top German officers, and he probably didn't care much for Jews. Nevertheless, he did use his influence, and it did not take long before the necessary papers found their way to the Euterpe Street HQ. From one day to the next my sister and I were suddenly taken off the list of deportees.

As an extra precaution, my mother did something else as well. She had abandoned the Catholic faith when she was eighteen, when the priest began prying, asking her indiscreet questions. On her way home from church, weeping, she had yelled, 'dirty pervert', and had never set foot in church again. But now she decided that her children should become Catholic as soon as possible.

To that end, we had to go to Waterlooplein Square once a week for catechism lessons from the father at the Moses and Aaron Church. We were each given a beautiful leather-bound, gilt-edged catechism book, with a silk bookmark-ribbon. Beyond that I don't remember much of those lessons, only the white lie we had to tell; the explanation we were given did not satisfy me, and I was quite bewildered by it, especially since my father wasn't supposed to know about these little excursions. Was it just a white lie if I had to make up some excuse, if he asked me where we were going? That would be telling a lie, in my book, and I didn't want to tell lies.

But the problem never presented itself since he never asked, and besides, the catechism lessons did not last very long.

The church was located in the Jewish quarter, the *Judenviertel*. That area was repeatedly being blocked off for yet another *razzia*, or round-up. My mother decided we had better stop going to the priest. Not long after that, the entire quarter was declared off-limits to non-Jews.

Meanwhile my father had found out about my mother's visit to Euterpe Street HQ. It started yet another furious argument, but he could foresee that she was going to stick to her guns no matter what, and by the start of the Christmas vacation we were allowed to remove the Star of David from our clothes, and I stopped attending the Jewish Lyceum.

11

My mother did try to warn her in-laws by sharing the information she was getting with them. The Germans were forcing the Jews living in the western part of the country to move to Amsterdam, to facilitate the deportations. There were enough empty homes for them to move into; their former Jewish occupants had already been deported. All the members of my father's family now lived in Amsterdam. My father's brother, Uncle Jacques, arrived from Haarlem with his wife. From The Hague came his sister Greta, with her husband and two youngest children, my cousins Betsy and Meta. Their eldest daughter Siphra came too with her husband and their baby. The fourth daughter, Chrisje, was already gone. When she'd received her summons, she had hurriedly married her fiancé, who would not let her go to Camp Westerbork alone, and my uncle had insisted on their getting married before leaving together.

We spent a good deal of time together in those days, Deetje, Meta and I. At the Girls' Lyceum, which I started at the beginning of 1943, after the Christmas holidays, I hadn't yet made any friends.

One day as I walked down Rijn Street with my two cousins,

a young man came up to me. He said, 'Hey, how come you're not wearing a star?'

It was Bernhard, the brother of Resi, our next-door neighbours on the Willemsparkweg, for whom I had stolen plums from the greengrocer's.

Before I had a chance to reply, he asked, 'So, where are you living these days?'

He looked at the stars on the coats of my two cousins. He had once intimidated me, but now I felt only a profound dislike rising in me. 'Oh, I live somewhere in the neighbourhood,' I said and hurriedly dragged my cousins around the corner, into Amstel Lane, where we began to run, swerving into Vecht Street. Only then did I dare peer cautiously around the corner to see if he had followed us.

After the war I heard that he had been an informant for the Germans. In the Café de Paris on Beethoven Street, he would mingle with the patrons and engage them in quasi-chummy conversations. He betrayed dozens of Jews that way. After the war he was given a twenty-year prison sentence.

Not long after their move to Amsterdam, Siphra and Alex too were transported to Westerbork with their baby. Betsy and Meta tried to make their parents feel better by writing them a poem on St Nicholas eve, which said, 'No matter how far away they may be, G'd* will watch over them.'

Siphra and Alex's baby died in Westerbork. Alex had already been sent on transport to Germany. Siphra was sent on to Auschwitz, where she died on 3 September 1943.

Betsy and Meta had no inkling of this, but on that

---

*Observant Jews avoid writing the name 'God' because of the risk that it might be defaced or destroyed. Here the letter 'o' was replaced with an apostrophe.

December day, as they wrote those words of consolation to their parents, their sister Chrisje and her husband had already been dead for several months. Gassed upon arrival in Auschwitz on 30 September.

Some years after the war my mother gave me a photograph album. It had been entrusted to her when the relatives from The Hague left. In it was a photo that was to acquire a special significance many years later.

In the 1990s I met an old man at the home of some friends. He told me that he was from Heerde, a small town in Gelderland. I asked him if he had always lived there. 'Born and bred,' he replied.

'A cousin of mine married a man with the same name as yours before the war,' I told him. 'He came from Heerde. Was he by any chance related to you? They were deported during the war with their baby and never returned. His name was Alex.'

'That's my brother.'

He took his wallet out of his breast pocket and took out an old, tattered photograph.

I knew that picture. I had the same one at home. Pasted in the old photograph album. It was the wedding photo of my cousin Siphra and Alex. I had been there myself, at that wedding.

'And that's my sister,' he said, pointing to one of the four bridesmaids in the picture.

When I had first received the album from my mother, I had wondered who the fourth bridesmaid was in that picture. I remembered Alex as a cheerful young man, but I apparently had not paid much attention to his relatives at the time.

The other three bridesmaids were the bride's sisters, my cousins Chrisje, Betsy and Meta.

'I am the only one in our family who survived the war,' he said, 'and I always carry this photo with me.'

Both of my father's youngest brothers, Jacques and Louis, were also ordered to report with their spouses to the Hollandse Schouwburg Theatre, which from the start of the war had been renamed the 'Jewish Theatre', serving as a venue for theatrical performances by Jewish actors for Jewish audiences. This theatre was now the point of assembly where transports to Westerbork were drawn up.

And that spring, Deetje departed for Westerbork with her parents.

I came home from school one day not long after that to find a note addressed to me in the hall: 'Hurry over to the Tugelaweg, they've been called up.' I never ran so fast in my life. When I came in, Uncle Maurits was busy burning holes in all the furniture with a lit cigarette: the Krauts weren't going to have the pleasure of enjoying his furnishings unscathed.

'You'll all be gassed, you mustn't go, you have to go into hiding!' I heard my mother say. But my uncle brushed aside her warnings, saying she was over-reacting. This led to quite a hullabaloo, for my mother refused to give up so easily. But they decided to go anyway; if they went into hiding and were discovered, their identity papers would be stamped with an S-mark, meaning they'd be singled out for special punishment, which was quite another matter than simply being sent to work in a German labour camp. As an S-offender, you were hardly given anything to eat and you were worked until you dropped.

I didn't understand what my mother meant when she said 'gassed'. It made me think, somehow, of pest control.

I walked over to my cousin Meta. We stopped listening to the adults' argument. With our arms around each other we stared at the burn-holes in the furniture. We thought it was a shame.

Their rucksacks were packed and ready to go in the hall. They were to go that evening. My father cried as he hugged his sister. I hurriedly slipped out the door.

Deetje and her parents were still in Westerbork when Maurits's family got there, and the two families arrived together in Sobibor on 11 June 1943; and there, on the very same day, Meta, Betsy, Deetje and their parents were all gassed.

My father, too, received a summons to report for deportation. His travel bag was ready in the hall. But fortunately the day of his departure kept being postponed, until the day came when he could stop wearing the star. My mother's intervention therefore also saved my father.

It wasn't until October 1943 that my father no longer had to wear the Star of David on his coat. The Germans had initiated a sterilisation program for Jews married to 'Aryan' spouses, so that Jews in mixed marriages would no longer be able to procreate. There were some doctors who foiled this measure by signing false affidavits that they had performed the surgery. My father was able to get hold of such an affidavit, which meant he no longer had to wear the star.

In the previous months we had, on a regular basis, been seeing long lines of Jews with knapsacks and bags walking along the streets, herded by German soldiers brandishing rifles. It usually took place in the evening or at night, after the general curfew, when everyone was off the streets.

One evening I heard the Germans screaming orders in our quiet street. Then I heard a cry. I jumped out of bed. From my bedroom window I could see the military truck parked on Lek Street. A young woman was being pushed into the back of the lorry while a man who was trying to stop her from being taken was roughly pulled back. The truck drove off. The man was left standing on the pavement, stunned.

Forty years after the war, I was browsing in the book section of the Bijenkorf department store in Amsterdam. Next to me stood an elderly man. We were both leafing through the same book about Sobibor.

Suddenly he spoke to me. 'My wife died there,' he said. 'We were living on Lek Street and she was taken away by the Germans. She was so young. We were newlyweds, we'd been married just before the race laws were issued making such a marriage illegal. I went to the SD headquarters on Euterpe Street to plead with them to let her go. I got into a fight. I was kicked and beaten. "*Judenfreund*" they cried after me as I stumbled out the door, bloodied. My tibia was broken.'

'Did you ever marry again?' I asked, curious. I was secretly hoping for some kind of happy ending.

'No, I never remarried,' he replied. 'I could not forget her.'

I put my hand on the arm of this stranger, and we stood there for a few seconds staring into each other's eyes, there in the middle of the busy book department of the Bijenkorf. Moments later we were back in the crowd, going our separate ways.

Soon there were no longer any Jews to be seen in the city. They were all either deported or in hiding. Another person we never heard from again was Hettie, my mother's seamstress-helper, after the fateful morning when she had come to tell us, with big, frightened eyes, that she had received the dreaded summons to report for deportation.

12

In January of 1943, after the Christmas holidays, I went with my father to the Girls' Lyceum to be registered as a second-form student. On the stairs, on our way to the headmistress's office, we met a little blonde girl. She stared at the Star of David which my father still wore on his coat. Then she looked at me. She smiled. I hoped she would be in my class; but, in the administrative office I asked about Adrie, my friend from primary school. So they put me in Adrie's class, and when we came home I phoned her excitedly and asked her to show me around my new school.

I rang her doorbell the next day. We had lost sight of each other, largely owing to the fact that as a Jew I wasn't allowed to go to her house; and since then she had not made an effort to contact me. She handed me a list with the names of all the kids in her class. She also pointed out which children in the class were Dutch Nazis. Her little brother came into the room. He saw me sitting there and cried, 'Jew!' Surely I must have misheard that, I thought to myself, but then I saw Adrie going all red in the face. I gathered that they had talked about me; the child must have overheard something.

For the first half of the war I had been a Jewish girl. Now I wasn't Jewish anymore. At the Girls' Lyceum nobody spoke about what was happening to the Jews in Amsterdam. I didn't talk about it either. The anti-Jewish measures I had been confronted with over the past two years had left me with a feeling of inferiority. I'd had to go to a special school; I had not been allowed to set foot inside any park, zoo, cinema, sports club, library, reading room or museum; we weren't allowed to travel; I wasn't allowed to ride my bike, I wasn't allowed to be outside after eight p.m., and I wasn't even allowed to just sit down on a public bench somewhere. That last restriction especially, and having to wear the Star of David, were the two most humiliating things to me. And I was beginning to believe I really was inferior.

Now I was having trouble adapting to my new situation. From time to time someone would ask me, 'What school did you come from?' Then I'd say, 'From the Jewish Lyceum.' But I didn't like telling them that. I felt ill at ease and out of place at this new school.

Our history teacher noticed this. She asked to see me and told me, 'You know, you can tell me anything.' It made me feel good that she understood what I was going through, but I couldn't bring myself to talk about what was happening at home and in my environment. It was just too absurd, too unreal, especially in this very different world. It did feel liberating to know that I myself didn't have to fear being deported, but at the same time it was depressing to think that almost all of my former friends and acquaintances were gone, and that many members of my own family too had disappeared.

Adrie had acquired a new group of friends in the interim. Her circle included one of the Dutch Nazi girls.

I did not make any new friends, and became very withdrawn.

After my intimate friendship with Anne at the Jewish Lyceum and its atmosphere of shared bonds, it was just too great a change for me.

While at the Girls' Lyceum, however, I did remain in contact with two girls from the Jewish Lyceum: Nannie and Hannah. It turned out that by 1943 they were the only ones from my former class who were left.

Hannah's father worked in the offices of the Jewish Council. The Council had been set up by the occupiers in order that they might be the ones to inform their own people of the latest measures issued by the enemy. The Jewish Council was also charged with seeing to it that those measures were implemented as peacefully as possible. Many people did anything they could to get a job in that office. It was a way to receive a deferment for deportation. So there was never any shortage of manpower there.

That was how my former classmate's father kept getting deferments. But one day when I arrived at her house, the entire family had just been taken away. The neighbours were standing on the pavement outside, talking excitedly. A woman next door told me that she had begged to be allowed to keep the little sister with her, but to no avail.

At home I thought it best to say nothing about it. My parents had enough worries of their own. They had just received word that Uncle Arie, my father's last remaining brother, had also been taken from his house. Notwithstanding the fact that he was in a mixed marriage, he had been arrested for ignoring some regulation.

Now Nannie was my only remaining link with the Jewish Lyceum. She was from a nice family and I liked going over to her house. I also liked her brother a lot. Her mother had a British passport and that seemed to offer the family some sort of protection. So they didn't think it was necessary to go into hiding.

The way in which I came to discover one evening that the entire family had been hauled off anyway, was very traumatic to me. I rang the doorbell. A neighbour saw me and told me in a very nonchalant tone of voice, 'All taken away, all taken away.' He said it twice. The no-nonsense manner in which he informed me of this, without any sort of emotion, totally discombobulated me. That was when I realised how indifferent some people's attitudes were to the deportations. I walked home miserably, trying to hold back my tears.

Both girls survived the camps. They returned to Amsterdam exhausted and sick. One of them returned with her sister, the other one had lost her entire family. I visited both of them. One of them was being cared for at the Joodse Invalide in Amsterdam, an institution which was now set up to receive and accommodate those who returned from the camps; the other was in a sanatorium outside the city. A great gulf had come between us, which was healed only years later: I had not gone through what they had gone through. I felt it as a reproach.

On my way to school I often thought about Anne. I missed her. On 6 July 1943 I noted that it was exactly a year since she had suddenly vanished from my life. I did not fit in at the new school and felt very lonely. I dreamed about the time when she would return from Switzerland and we'd be able to resume our friendship where we'd left off.

The following year I also commemorated July 6. I had made new friends by that time, but I was still very focused on that date.

I wasn't able to tell her father how much I had missed

her until many years later, years and years after the war. Hearing this pleased him very much. He was just as much of an extrovert as his daughter, while I was still as reserved as ever. Since I hardly ever spoke of it, there had been no way for him to know that after her departure she was so frequently in my thoughts. That was when he let me read Anne's original, plaid-covered diary, which he kept in a safe-deposit box in Basel. I had been too shy to ask.

I thought about my other classmates from the Jewish Lyceum and my cousins too, but in quite a different way. Of my cousins and Hannah and Nannie, I knew they had been deported. I didn't know which of the others were in hiding. As certain as I was at that time that I would see Anne again after the war, I was quite in the dark about the fate of the other kids.

During my 'Jewish' war years, until 1943, the world around me grew increasingly restricted. Ours was a very small circle, and we relied on each other completely, since the German decrees banned all outside influences. It was safer to head directly home after school, and besides school, we did not stray far from our homes.

After that, my world did open up a bit. I was able to visit Amsterdam's other neighbourhoods again, such as the Beethoven quarter, where the Girls' Lyceum was located. It was something of a relief, but it still didn't make me feel free.

At the end of the school year I had a very bad report card. I would have to repeat the second form. After the summer holidays I started again in a new class. I felt more at ease there, and to my delight the sweet little blonde I had met on the stairs when I was first registering at the school was in this class. Grietje and I sat next to each other.

Anne and Grietje could not have been more different:

Anne, who was always trying to probe the deepest places in my heart; and Grietje, who came from a farming family from Groningen, and who considered my reserve as something mysterious and exotic, which was what attracted her about me. I valued her down-to-earth nature and her practical intelligence. We spent quite a bit of time together, even though she lived on the east side of Amsterdam, at Watergraafs Lake, which was a half-hour walk from my house. She always had a solution to everything and gave me excellent advice whenever I had to make a decision about something. She had her own set of friends in her neighbourhood, and I had mine locally as well. My friendship with her was less close than my friendship with Anne, but it was an easy, relaxed sort of friendship.

Through the years we remained good friends and kept in touch, even if we didn't see each other for long periods of time when one of us lived abroad.

I became a member of the hockey club to which another girl in my class belonged, and played tennis with Cox, a girl at my school who lived on Rijn Street, around the corner from where I lived on Hunze Street. Cox was in the same form but another class, and she once hailed me in the middle of the road, as we were both crossing Rijn Street.

'You're at the Girls' Lyceum too, aren't you?' she asked, rather shyly.

From that time on we walked to school together. We always met at the statue of Wilhelmina Drucker ('Women, keep the torch burning!') at the north end of Amstel Lane. After a while, Ina, a girl who was in the classical branch of our school joined us; she lived on Waal Street. If one of us was late and we didn't feel like waiting any longer, we'd write our initials on the pavement, which did pose a bit of a problem if there was a downpour.

A couple of years later I was elected to the school's student council together with Ina. We took the initiative to set up a reading room with books and magazines in a vacant room on the ground floor of the building, where I, for one, spent much of my time instead of doing my homework. We hung current class photos on the walls, and notices to our fellow students. Ina came up with the name 'The Librije', which was painted on the door in flowing cursive letters. The deputy headmaster, who seemed to get quite a kick out of our enterprise, kept an eye on us; at least, he kept coming round and peeking inside. But he may have had quite a different motive instead, as I was to find out later.

During those years we progressed from *Peter Rabbit* to Shakespeare's *Hamlet* in English class, and in German from *Die Biene Maja* to Goethe's *Faust*. Grietje knew why we were better at English than at German: 'It's just because we have a much better teacher, it has nothing to do with us.' I wanted to believe her, but I myself thought it also had to do with the fact that we felt more attracted to English at that time.

In French we learned poetry by heart and we read *Le Grand Meaulnes*. We also had accounting lessons, which were given by former world chess champion Max Euwe, who was attached to our school as maths teacher for the gymnasium side. I also loved the art classes at this school; I was more inclined to draw flowers these days. One other girl and I were granted permission to come and paint under the art teacher's supervision after school.

In Dutch class we were rereading *Camera Obscura* and Multatuli; *Kees de jongen* was a new addition. The Dutch teacher told us about the deaths of Menno ter Braak and Eddy du Perron in May 1940. It was clear that their deaths had affected her greatly. We didn't read their books until the war was over. The actor Eduard Verkade was an acquaintance of hers. He once came to school to perform Hamlet's monologue. He was an old man, but I noticed that during the performance he suddenly became the young Hamlet.

I didn't devote much effort to my homework, neither in language nor in maths, physics or chemistry, but I did manage to move up to the next form every year. The war ended as I was graduating from the fourth to the fifth form of the Girls' Lyceum.

13

For the rest of the war we lived for news of the Allied forces, news which was hard to come by, and was beginning to sound more and more optimistic. The Nazi-censored radio broadcasts, of course, only brought news of their own victories.

The sooner the war was over, the greater the chance that relatives and friends would return from Germany safe and sound; at least that's what we thought. We did not yet know, or, rather, could not imagine, that upon arrival in Auschwitz or Sobibor, where many of the transports out of Westerbork were heading, most of the Jews were sent straight to the gas chambers and had long since perished.

At school everyone cautiously steered clear of the subject of the war and the Resistance. In our class there were some students whose parents were known to be with the Dutch Nazis. There were also teachers whom we did not trust. Some teachers resisted quietly by leaving the prescribed textbooks, written from a propagandistic point of view, unopened; in history class, for example. People suspected our geography teacher of being in the Resistance, but nobody spoke of it openly.

He was the one who had arrived at school greatly agitated on the morning of 24 October 1944, when on my way to school I had seen the smouldering remains of two villas at the corner of the Apollo Lane. An officer of the SD, the infamous Oehlschlägel, operating from his desk on Euterpe Street and known to be responsible for the deaths of many Dutch citizens, had been liquidated by the Resistance. In retaliation, twenty-nine members of the Resistance had been dragged out of the Weteringschans prison that morning and executed at the site of that murder – among them were twelve men who had been picked up in the Rivers quarter; some of whom had been in hiding to avoid being sent to work in the German war industry, and some who had been illegal workers. To set an example, the Germans had left the bodies lying there for several hours. They had also set fire to the two villas. Our teacher had passed by there early that morning and had seen the whole thing.

He was also the one who saw to it that at the end of the last winter of the war, there would be hot soup for the students.

There continued to be *razzias* from time to time, to root out any hidden Jews. When it was a matter of betrayal (there was a monetary reward for every Jew reported, and we soon came to realise that this was a temptation even for people who had no sympathy with the Nazi regime), there usually was no time to escape, especially not in Amsterdam.

A distant relative of ours twice fled to our house in a panic. He knew that he would be safe with us in case of need. I barely knew him and stared at him from a corner of the hall, at his hounded, frightened eyes. I was frightened myself; the Germans were still in the area, the house searches were still going on and it was known that our family was half-Jewish – that was the reason my mother did not want to shelter anyone in our house. The Germans could have stormed into our house at any moment; but that never happened.

When it grew dark, the relative disappeared again, hoping that his benefactors at his previous address would help him find a new place to hide.

Resistance organisations to help Jews find shelter sprang up during the second half of the war. They provided forged papers, ration cards and hiding places. It wasn't usually possible for families to go into hiding together. A Jewish boy who lived across the street from us on Hunze Street had abruptly disappeared in March of 1943. After the war he came back. He had been hidden and was now returning to his old neighbourhood.

In the little village community were he had been lying low for over two years, separated from his own family, it had been important not to draw attention to himself by any unusual behaviour. He was supposed to be a nephew of the couple who had taken him in, and he called them 'Uncle' and 'Aunt'. Every Sunday he would go with them to church.

One Sunday, before the sermon began, the pastor announced from the pulpit, 'I must warn you that at the end of the service there will be a checkpoint outside. It would be best if those who think this might affect them leave the church right now.' It was a brave and dangerous announcement.

It was 1944. The longer the war went on, the more German men were called up for military duty. Workers employed in the arms factories were drafted into the army and replaced by men from the German-occupied territories. If you wanted to avoid this conscription, you had to go into hiding. The pastor's warning was primarily directed at those men.

Several young men got to their feet and left the church. They were largely students who had fled to this remote region and now worked as farmhands in the fields.

But our fourteen-year-old neighbour thought the warning

was also for him. He glanced anxiously at his aunt and made as if to stand up. She, however, pushed him back down onto the bench and hissed, 'Sit down. If you get up now, everyone here will know you're Jewish!' Petrified, with a hammering heart, he sat through the service.

When the service was over, they stepped outside. Sure enough, there they were, six German soldiers, guns drawn. They were in the process of rounding up men they deemed sufficiently fit to be sent to work in the German factories. The men were ordered to line up, and were subsequently marched off.

The boy walked past the German soldiers, unnoticed, and arrived home safely with his 'aunt'.

Food rations became increasingly meagre. Even with our ration cards we often had to queue up for ages to wait our turn outside the shops, hoping to get something before everything was gone. Once the 'hunger winter' of 1944–45 began, it grew harder and harder to find anything to eat in the big cities. If the baker announced that he would sell bread the next day, we would queue up at the crack of dawn for a soggy loaf of bread, which would have to last a long time. You saw exhausted people slouched in doorways, unable to go any farther. Many of them suffered from hunger oedema; you could tell from their swollen legs.

Several times a week we'd walk to Roelof Hart Square and back, where we were given a plate of the German military's leftovers, which had been earmarked for schoolchildren. We usually found it quite edible; we weren't used to much any more, but sometimes we were given soup made of potato peels, which I couldn't stomach. Towards the end, there was nothing but tulip bulbs and sugar beets to be had for the people of Amsterdam. For huge sums of money, or by going into the countryside and visiting farms (riding a bike without tyres, since there was no rubber, or pushing a wheelbarrow or pram), you could sometimes score a few potatoes or some beans. Scarce necessities, such as linens, soap or matches, could be traded to a farmer for food. As well as jewellery, of course.

Gas and electricity were shut off and we cooked on a little primus stove that didn't use much fuel. But it didn't heat the room either. We went to bed early in order not to feel the cold. The oil lamp that served as our light gave off a lot of black smoke and a nasty smell, without providing much illumination.

I came to know a boy at my hockey club who paid a great deal of attention to me. I felt flattered. His name was Thijs. He was the captain of his team. After we had gone skating together one time, he escorted me home and went upstairs with me. It was the middle of the hunger winter. All we had was a bag of dried beans, which my mother would frugally cook up for us a couple of times a week.

In those days a cousin of Deetje's father often came to our house with her husband, always towards dinner time. They would warm themselves by the primus stove, which was lit to cook the beans, and ate with us. They were starving. In their hiding place there was nothing left to eat, and their money was gone. I would sometimes see them sneak a bean from the pan. After supper they would always leave again, for some address unknown.

That evening they happened to be there too. As I entered the room with Thijs, he glanced at where they were sitting in semi-darkness and asked softly, 'Are those Jews?' I was startled. The meaning of the little white lie finally dawned on me. I said, 'No.' It was obvious that he did not believe me.

I don't know if they heard, but our dinner company never returned to our house again after that episode.

Neither did Thijs. He didn't want to get mixed up with any Jews, he said.

It was April 1945. The liberation of the western part of the Netherlands was near, but there was such a lack of food in the cities that more and more people were dying of starvation. There were no food deliveries any more. The Allies decided to start air-dropping provisions over the city.

We were in class one day when we heard planes overhead. The entire school ran upstairs to the roof. We waved scarves and handkerchiefs at the pilots from the free world, our friends, and we saw a cloud of black dots drifting down over a field on the outskirts of the city.

There was a villa across the canal from us where a number of German officers were housed. We saw them staring at us through their windows. After watching our delirium for a while, they stormed angrily to the headmistress's office and ordered us off the roof.

The planes were the precursors of liberation, which came a few weeks later.

14

On 5 May 1945 Germany's capitulation was now a reality. On my way to Grietje's house I saw handbills posted on the Ring Dyke proclaiming that fact. The handbills also warned that the Canadians would not be arriving in Amsterdam until 7 May. The liberators themselves were nowhere yet to be seen.

There lived a man on Rijn Street who had ignored the German order to hand in his radio. He had now placed his receiver on the windowsill, where it broadcast the latest news at top volume. People flocked over there to listen to the good news. I did too.

But the Germans had not yet gone. Suddenly a little band of German soldiers walked up. Silently they aimed their guns at us. We scattered in a panic, getting in each other's way. But they did not fire. Their silence gave the situation an air of sinister unreality.

Later we heard that there had been shooting at the Dam Square. A girl in our hockey club had been in the crowd celebrating the liberation there and was shot dead, along with some other unfortunates. The bullets were fired from a building in which German officers were billeted in the war, and where they were now waiting out whatever would come next.

The Canadians who were to liberate us in Amsterdam were on their way, and at school we promptly learned to sing the Canadian national anthem, so that we'd be able to serenade our liberators. I still remember it: *Oh, Canada, with glowing hearts we see thee rise, Our true North strong and free!* The words 'glowing hearts' and 'free' expressed our feelings exactly. Joy and freedom. The world was open to us again.

In our old, threadbare clothes we gathered on Berlage Bridge to wait for the Canadians – Cox, Ina and myself. When they finally arrived, they hoisted us into their jeeps and onto their lorries. There was much cheering and clapping. We drove with them to Vondelpark, where they pitched their tents and handed out tins of food, chocolate and cigarettes.

Later we had to walk home the whole way. But walking was something we were used to, it had been such a long time since we had had bicycles or public transportation. On the way back we munched on the chocolate, another thing we hadn't had for so long.

There were many homes that were empty; they belonged to the deported Jews. In our own street, too, there were abandoned houses. Of the seventeen thousand Jews who had lived in the Rivers Quarter shortly before the war, we learned after the war, almost thirteen thousand had been murdered.

At the end of the war, a boy and his mother who had been evacuated from the coast had come to live in one of the houses next door. We seemed to bump into each other in the street so often that it couldn't really have been a coincidence. It was with this boy that I wildly celebrated the liberation.

Committees were formed in every neighbourhood to organise all sorts of festivities. At first I went with my girlfriends, but once Pieter came on the scene we had eyes only for each other. We trailed from one street party to the next and danced until late in the night to the American music. When the weather was nice we went on excursions to the Bosplan, now called the Amsterdam Woods, with picnic baskets. The liberation revelry lasted all summer long.

Pieter's mother, a young widow, was happy that he had found someone to hang out with. She had plunged herself into the whirl of the liberation and spent much time in the company of the Canadians, who had stayed on in Amsterdam in large numbers. 'My sister is not at home,' I heard him tell a Canadian officer who rang the doorbell one day. He was backing his mother's story; she had not told the Canadians that she had a seventeen-year-old son at home.

Pieter introduced me to his circle of friends. He knew I had a Jewish father, but he didn't talk about it with his friends; neither did I. So they made no effort to refrain from making constant anti-Semitic remarks in my presence such as, 'Look, there goes a Jew again,' or some gossip about a Jew who had had the nerve to come back and demand the return of the silver which he had entrusted to the neighbours for safekeeping.

I would say nothing at all. It made me think of that history lesson when I was at the Jewish Lyceum, when the teacher had unexpectedly launched into a diatribe about the Spanish Inquisition. Just as I had then, I felt terribly uncomfortable, an outsider above all.

I began to back off a bit. I went less and less often to street festivals with Pieter, instead I let myself be dragged along by a boy my father liked me to go out with and who had been pursuing me in vain all summer. I thought he was a very nice boy, but that was all. Pieter would not accept this, and he broke up with me.

Grietje went to the parties in her own neighbourhood, in East Amsterdam, and sometimes I would go with her. One night I spotted Thijs, for he lived there too. Suddenly I could not imagine how I could ever have been in awe of him. I looked the other way. As did he.

Before school began again in the autumn, Cox, Ina and I took Cox's father's Canadian canoe on a paddling trip down the River Vecht. We christened the boat with a new name in honour of the Canadians who had set us free: *Liberator*.

After the initial jubilation came the disenchantment. Food supplies had started trickling in again, but at the same time the first news reports of the camps came dribbling out, and of the state in which the Allies had found the survivors when they came to liberate them. That which we had hardly been able to believe during the war, turned out to be all too true. Until I saw the first photographs and film clips of the liberation of the concentration camps with my own eyes, I could not even imagine it.

Jenny, the daughter of a friend of my father's, was the first to return from Auschwitz, and came directly to our house. There was no one whom she knew left in Amsterdam. Later it transpired that neither her parents, nor just about the entire remainder of her family would ever return. She threw herself into my mother's arms, weeping. She had a camp number tattooed on her arm. That night she told my parents everything, all the horrors she had experienced. She was only a year older than me. She would live with us for the time being.

We waited to see if other relatives or friends would come back, but there was an eerie silence. The Red Cross, which during the war had not concerned itself much with the fate of the Jews, now came up with lists of names. They were lists that had been neatly kept by the Nazis to keep track of the Jews they had exterminated, with the place and time. My father went every day to look at the lists that had come in and that were posted in various locations around the city, including Central Station, the Social Services and the Joodse Invalide, and every day he only found more confirmation that nobody in his family was likely to ever come back. My uncles and aunts, Deetje and Meta and my other cousins were all dead.

For my father it was difficult to pick up the pieces again. His entire family had been annihilated. On top of that, although the official Jew-baiting had now been repealed, the war and Nazi propaganda had had the effect of stirring up anti-Semitism in the Netherlands, and that was quite noticeable after the war. My sister and I had had such personal experiences with it ourselves that, now that we had the choice, we were not interested in becoming Jewish once more. For my father, who in contrast became very observant after the war, it must have been a bitter blow. The relationship between him and my mother had not improved in those difficult years of the war. He now regularly attended the synagogue and spent much of his time with the handful of Jewish friends who were left.

From Anne I heard not a word. I did think it was rather strange. Suddenly, out of the blue, her father rang our doorbell. Seeing him gave me a shock: sad eyes, thin face, his threadbare suit hanging loosely on his emaciated frame. And he was alone. I was very puzzled until he told us his story, and the terrible truth dawned on us. They had not gone to Switzerland, but had been hidden for over two years behind his office on the Prinsengracht canal, with the Van Pels family, consisting of the father, mother and son Peter, and Pfeffer, the dentist. They had been betrayed and transported to Westerbork, and from there on to Poland, on the last transport. The men and women had been separated early on. He had arrived in Auschwitz with Peter van Pels and had been there for months.

When the Allies were on their way, Mr Frank had stayed behind in the infirmary barracks, but Peter was marched off in the opposite direction by the Germans, heading back to Germany. It became clear later that practically none of the inmates on this 'death march' ever returned, Peter among them. Mr Frank was freed by the Russians on 27 January 1945. After a period of recovery to regain some of his strength, he started on his homeward journey to the Netherlands on 5 March. He took the train from Odessa to Marseilles, and from there he sailed to Amsterdam on board a ship. He arrived on 3 June.

He moved in with Miep and Jan Gies, and he informed us about the role Miep had played in taking care of the eight hidden residents of the Prinsengracht. Miep and Jan Gies at that time lived across from us on Hunze Street. We had seen Mrs Gies walking past our house all through the war years, and we knew that she used to work in Mr Frank's office, but we had never suspected a connection between her and the Frank family's disappearance. The note they had left behind about going to Switzerland had done its job. Suddenly I understood where the chairs in their Merwedeplein home had disappeared to.

Once he was back, Mr Frank often came over to our house. He had already heard that his wife Edith had died, but he had no news as yet of Margot and Anne, and he still clung to the hope that they had survived the camp. He kept going back to check the lists, meanwhile asking any of the few survivors who had returned from the camps if they could give him any news of his daughters. Jenny, who still lived with us at the time, told him that she had seen Margot and Anne in her camp, Auschwitz, just before it was liberated. But there was no way she could have. Anne and Margot, it turned out, had been in Auschwitz for only a brief period, and they had actually died in March, in Bergen-Belsen. Jenny's story gave Mr Frank false hope. But that hope had soon flown, for even before he had seen their names on one of the lists, he was put in touch with a nurse who, with her sister, had been with them when first Margot, and the next day Anne, had died. 'How do you tell a father that both of his daughters are dead?' I was to hear her say later. I couldn't understand how Jenny could have done something like that to him. He was sobbing when he came over to tell me.

Miep was unable to save Anne's life, but she did save her diary. Anne had been keeping the diary from her birthday on 12 June 1942, until the day she was arrested, on 4 August 1944. Miep found that first diary, with its tartan cover, in the abandoned back rooms on Prinsengracht, and also the accounts ledgers and loose sheets of paper which Anne had filled with her reworked version. She'd meant to give everything back to Anne when she returned. When she was sure that Anne was dead, she handed it over, without reading it, to Mr Frank.

He came to our house almost every day, and talked to me about what Anne did while in hiding or in Westerbork, the Dutch prison camp. In Westerbork she had gone so far as to declare herself delighted, because after two years of being shut in she could finally be outside again, in the sun.

He would bring me little gifts, for example a booklet explaining the text of the Mattheus Passion. He had come in and noticed me listening to it on the radio; he turned and walked out again, to return a little while later with the booklet.

It was obvious that it made him feel better to be able to talk about Anne with me. I think that it gave him the feeling that his connection with his daughter was not yet totally gone, because she lived on in my memory. He knew about our close friendship and he knew of Anne's feelings for me. Anne had often spoken of me while in hiding; she had talked about me with Miep, who was able to tell her about me since I lived across the street from her. And now Mr Frank was reading Anne's diary, in which he kept coming across my name, and which contained two letters that Anne had written to me from her hiding place. 'I think of you so often,' she'd written.

'Who would have thought it, of our Anne?' her father said to me, meaning the deep thoughts confided to her diary, which he related to me. But it didn't surprise me at all. When later I read the diary myself, I recognised much of the kind of preoccupation we used to have. Her belief in the innate goodness of people was something I used to share with her. But I have had to change my views on that over the years.

He often wept when he was with me. I didn't quite know how to deal with that. I was sixteen and in my eyes Mr Frank was an old man. On top of that, being confronted with Otto Frank's grief directly contravened my own post-war determination not to think of the dark times that lay behind me, or dwell on the loss of my relatives and friends. The fact that my happy, ebullient friend, with all her plans and ideals, had had to suffer the atrocities of the camps and was now dead, was to me an unimaginable thought. But I avoided talking about that with him. He himself kept returning to the subject of Anne the way she used to be, and he wanted me to tell him all about our friendship.

I was there when he needed me, and even reluctantly accompanied him into town when he asked me to. We would sit across from each other in various cafés, having lengthy conversations which he would steer in Anne's direction as often as he could.

One day he took me to the house on Prinsengracht where they had been hidden. In later years it was to become Amsterdam's most popular museum, surpassed in number of visitors only by the Rijksmuseum. He showed me the rooms where Anne had been shut in for all those years. I tried to imagine his feelings as he walked through those empty rooms that held so many sad memories for him. But he didn't let any of that show, although he was quieter than usual. I saw the papered-over windows, the small kitchen sink and the Delft-blue lavatory. And I saw the wall on which Anne had pasted the film stars and postcards we had collected and sorted together. Suddenly Anne seemed very close. It had been almost four years since we had cut out those pictures. But I remembered as if it was yesterday how happy we had been, and how we had refused to let the adults' problems spoil our fun. Now Anne was dead, but the thought of death had never occurred to us back then in 1942. Seeing those pictures, it seemed unimaginable to me all over again.

Among the postcards on the wall there were two of the two English princesses, Elizabeth and Margaret Rose. So had Anne had copies of those too, I wondered? In the summer of 1938 my sister and I had been given a four-card series of the British royals, when we visited Paris during the British King and Queen's official visit to France. But we did sometimes trade postcards, and when I found in my own collection a Shirley Temple postcard addressed to Margot Frank, I realised what must have happened. On further examining my collection, I found what I was looking for – the two remaining postcards. Were the missing two the same ones that were now pasted to the wall in the house on Prinsengracht?

Still, I felt that I wasn't doing nearly enough to help, compared with my mother, whom I overheard having long discussions with Otto about the camps. She did the same for others who were returning from the camps or coming out of hiding. Our home was open to all of them, and my mother lent a willing ear. They were broken, they had lost everything and everyone, and had to attempt to pick up the pieces of their lives again. My father would listen, but did not say much. My mother, on the other hand, talked a lot about the war and about the great tragedy that had taken place. She was outspoken in her outrage over the fate of her family and friends.

'I realise that I wasn't very supportive to you back then,' I would write to him years later.

From her place by the window, where she used to sit with her sewing, my mother had a good view of the entire street. At a certain time every day she would see a little old lady with lovely silvery-grey hair and clear blue eyes pass by. She always carried a violin case. My mother was intrigued, and one time, when she bumped into her in the street, she struck up a conversation with her. The two of them hit it off, and from then on this lady came to dinner at our house every Tuesday. She came from a musical Jewish family, and was full of stories. I would often stay home when she came over. Not to hear my mother's stories, which I already knew, but for this woman's anecdotes, which greatly entertained me. Such as the one about her father, who, when listening to a concert recital that did not please him, would always mouth the word 'atrocious' as if he were saying 'magnificent'. It became a favourite catchphrase in our home.

She would bring along the daughter of friends who had died in the war, and who had been left equally destitute, and some months later, she, in turn, brought along her new boyfriend. This young man had won a prize for a book he'd written, and she had met him at the prize-giving, where she herself had received an honourable mention for her book of sonnets.

My mother would fry up a batch of fish and set out a big bowl of boiled potatoes; there was always vegetable soup to start, and coffee after dinner. My mother didn't do dessert. And it didn't bother her that the whole house reeked of fried fish. Our guests didn't seem to mind either, because they continued to come every Tuesday evening.

I would always try to be home on those nights; now it was in order to hear the stories of the young author, and to talk with him. He had a very special sense of humour, which my sister did not appreciate, so she made sure never to be home when they came. I found the same sense of humour in his book, which I read. It made quite a stir, and received some good, but mostly critical, reviews. I kept bursting out laughing as I read it, but I couldn't understand how he could depict his parental home in the way that he did. What I thought was so clever was the way that the tedium and boredom described in the book led to so much suspense that the book itself wasn't dull at all.

I did not notice the tension that eventually arose between the two lovebirds, and I would not have understood it either.

They were permanent members of the artist's society, De Kring, and they told me about the assistant headmaster of my school, who was involved with one of our teachers. The young writer's choice of words in telling this story sent me into gales of laughter, notwithstanding my embarrassment.

At school I didn't mention what I had heard, not even to Grietje, Cox or Ina, but from that time on the sparks of intimacy between the assistant head and the teacher did not escape my notice. And I was leery when not long afterwards my name would appear almost daily on the noticeboard in the main hall, ordering me to the assistant headmaster's office after school. He taught Latin and Greek and I was not in any of his classes. I only knew him from his visits to our Librije. I would just hover near the door every time; he would order me to shut it, and then he'd stare at me from behind his desk, saying, 'Well, well!' I said nothing in return, gazed at him wide-eyed and refused to return his smile. Nothing else was said, and he would then nod that I could go. When after a week of this he had failed to get anywhere with me, the summons on the noticeboard stopped. He had apparently been waiting for some sign of encouragement from me.

15

$\mathbf{M}$r Frank gave me a copy of the two letters that Anne had written to me from her hiding place. In September 1942 she had copied them into her diary, adding the words, 'as you probably already knew'. It was the promised 'letter of farewell' that he had found in her diary, together with a second letter to me that she had written subsequently. She had not been allowed to leave the farewell letter in the abandoned house on Merdeweplein Square; she had started writing it when she heard she was going to go into hiding. In her second letter she thanked me for my reply. I never did reply, however, since I never received the farewell letter. I spent the entire war assuming that she was safe and sound in Switzerland. She had simply made up my answer to her, and she was replying in turn to this made-up letter.

This is the promised letter of farewell   *25 September 1942*

Dear Jacqueline,
I am writing you this letter to say goodbye, it will probably surprise you, but fate intends for it to be so, I have to leave (as you probably already know) with my family, you know the reason why.

*When you called me Sunday afternoon I couldn't tell you
anything, because my mother said I mustn't, the whole house
was already in an uproar, and the front door was locked.
Hello was going to come over to see me, but we didn't open
the door. I can't write to everybody, so I'll just write to you.
I assume that you won't tell anyone about this letter, or who
it came from. If you'd agree to have a secret correspondence
with me, I'd be ever so grateful. <u>Ask Mrs Gies!!!</u> I hope we'll
see each other again soon, but it probably won't be before
the war is over. If Lies* or anyone else asks if you ever hear
from me, never tell them that you have, because you'd be
putting Mrs Gies and the rest of us in mortal danger, and I
do hope you're sensible enough to recognise that. Eventually,
of course, you could just tell them that you'd had one letter
from me, to say goodbye. Well now Jackie, be well, I hope I'll
receive some sign of life from you very soon, and that we'll
see each other again shortly.*
Your '<u>best</u>' friend

Anne

*P.S. I hope that until we see each other again we'll always be
'<u>best</u>' friends.*

Byeyeyeye

<u>*Second Letter*</u>   *25 September 1942*

Dear Jackie,
*I was very happy to receive your letter, and if the Germans
haven't been in our house yet, you could go to Mr Goldschmith
and pick up some of our books and notebooks and games; you
can keep them or save them for me, or you could take them*

---

*Hannah, nicknamed Lies by her friends.

*over to Mrs Gies. I forgot to tell you in my last letter that
you <u>mustn't</u> save these letters, because <u>no one</u> must ever
find them. So tear them into tiny little snippets, the way we
did on the roof with my mother's carton. I hope you'll do
it. How are you all, I'm not allowed to tell you about me, of
course. I think of you so often. How is Ilse doing, is she still
with you? I heard from Mrs Gies that Lies is still around.
We're not bored, we have company, that's all I'm allowed to
say about our life, it's scary but interesting, for later. I'm
not allowed to make this letter too long, see you later and
a little kiss from*

Anne

When I found out that in hiding Anne had written letters to
the fictional friends of Joop ter Heul, whom she pretended
were her own friends, and that she had written a reply to a
letter of mine which she had never actually received, I was
extremely moved, and I felt terribly bad for her. How lonely
my friend must have felt in her claustrophobic hiding place,
among people who did not understand her at all!

But I also knew it was sensible of her father not to let
her have the 'secret correspondence' with me which she
proposed in her first letter. We were too young to take on
that kind of responsibility.

Otto Frank never wanted to talk about who might have
betrayed them. It could have been one of the people in the
warehouse downstairs. They had not been informed of the
hiding place in the annex, but it was clear from comments
they occasionally made that they did eventually find out
about it.

For years people have speculated about who was responsible. After two different hypotheses were put forward in

two recent biographies of Anne Frank, the NIOD began an investigation in 2002. There has not been sufficient proof for either theory.

Every now and then, Mr Frank would bring over one of the grey accounts books in which Anne had continued her diary when her first tartan journal was full. He gave it to my parents to read. I just glanced at it, but did not peruse it. I had looked for Anne's diary three years earlier at their Merwedeplein home to see what she had written about her friends. But now I considered it inappropriate that others were reading Anne's most intimate thoughts. My mother read the extracts Otto showed her with great interest. I realised only much later, when in an interview my mother referred to Anne and me as a pair of 'lovebirds', that these were mainly passages about me.

Upon receiving a copy of the first edition of *The Secret Annex* from Otto, I wrote to him on 28 June 1947: 'So finally her fondest wish has now been fulfilled, and your patience and all the trouble you went through rewarded.' In the introduction, by Annie Romein-Verschoor, the diary was compared to the then-famous diary of Marie Bashkirtseff, the Russian artist whose renown rested largely on her diaries. According to Annie Romein, Anne's diary, when compared to Bashkirtseff's coyness, was a wonder of authenticity.

I ended my letter with, 'Who knows, some day Anne's book could even become as famous as that.' I said that, really, to buck him up, because I didn't have much faith in it. It came as no surprise to me that the first publisher Otto Frank had approached had seen no particular merit in a young girl's musings, and thought it would be a losing proposition. On top of which, so soon after the war, people weren't at all interested in reading books about that war.

Anne's diary became famous the world over after a theatrical production and then a film was made of it in America. Anne became a legend, and so Anne's girlfriend Jopie, who was mentioned in the diary, became a part of that legend. For years I managed to hide behind the name Anne had invented for me, Jopie. I did not want to be constantly reminded of the war by Anne's diary. Nobody knew that I had been Anne's best friend, not even my acquaintances. Added to that was the fact that I did not want to be considered important or special just because I'd had a friend who had died in a concentration camp.

But as the diary's fame grew and I grew more and more reticent on the subject, I was startled by a dismaying phenomenon. Suddenly all kinds of people started to come out of the woodwork who professed to have known Anne, or to have been on intimate terms with her, even if this was far from the truth.

I knew how Anne would have reacted to this sort of thing. I felt I had to speak up for my friend who was no longer able to speak for herself, and I gave vent to my indignation.

I dislike being the centre of attention. That is why I practise my chosen career largely in the solitude of my studio – my interest in the history of books and the art of bookmaking led me to become a bookbinder: I design and create covers and bindings. Now, against my will, I was being drawn more and more into the limelight.

But I had meanwhile become aware of the important message spread by Anne's book, a message against discrimination. It shows where discrimination and prejudice can lead when carried out to the bitter end.

16

One year after the war, when the trains had started running again, my mother decided to visit her brother in Paris. She took me along, and it was the first time in seven years that we were in my grandparents' village again. Albert now lived in the house by himself. He had looked after his parents when they were ill, and had divided his time between them and his girlfriend, who lived in the city. He had spent most of the last years of the war in the village, where he had been a member of a resistance group that had been formed there.

The journey was tiring. We had to change trains at the border with all our luggage, and we had to wait a long time at customs. Since the River Seine traced a big loop near the village, the train from the Gare Saint Lazare to the village had to cross two railway bridges. But since the bridges over the Seine had been bombed in the war and were not yet repaired, we had to get off the train before the first bridge, lug our cases across a pedestrian bridge to the other side, get onto a bus, cross another pedestrian bridge, and then get back on a train on the other side waiting to take us to our destination.

Albert picked us up from the train in the delivery van

belonging to his chum, Chantal's father. Chantal had come along as well. We had parted as children, but now we were no longer kids.

It was an emotional reunion. Albert barely recognised me. 'How big you've grown,' he cried, a bit embarrassed. My mother and her brother were both in tears. As we drove into their street, I missed my grandparents' familiar faces. They used to lean over the terrace railing, on the lookout for our arrival. The chicken coop was empty, the weeds were rampant. The house was neglected too. I saw my mother gazing around, but she did not say anything.

Albert cooked a meal for us and over supper told his sister that he had decided to remain in the village permanently. He was planning to remarry, and bring his bride here. Even though my mother was not very fond of Jeanne and thought her brother would be marrying down in taking her as his wife, she assented to his plan. She loved her brother very much and thought it would be better for his health if he lived in the countryside. Moreover, she herself was emotionally attached to the house and the village, where her parents were now interred in the family grave in the old churchyard, and where she, too, hoped to be buried one day. My mother lived until 1992. She was 101 years old, and was buried in the Netherlands. She had not been back to the village in many years. Too much water under the bridge. She had outgrown her native country.

Albert took it for granted that he would live in the house under the same conditions as his parents had, and my mother did not protest. He would therefore only be responsible for the overhead expenses. They would share the cost of patching the roof, which was in serious need of repair. Albert told us that the cistern, which had always been the source of fresh water for the house, was no longer

potable; the tank had been polluted in the war by the guns
and munitions hidden inside by the Resistance.

Chantal came to pick me up shortly afterwards. Leaving
my mother and her brother to exchange sombre stories of
their war experiences, I was welcomed into Chantal's circle
of friends. In Amsterdam we had just finished celebrating
the first anniversary of our liberation; here, once again, I was
swept up in wild rejoicing, in this case a commemoration of
the liberation of Paris, on 25 August 1944. The festivities were
in full swing. Blue, white and red bunting hung everywhere,
and we trooped from one village to the next, wherever there
were street fairs and dancing until deep into the night. When
we were younger I had felt awkward in their company, but
now the boys from the villages were quite interested in
dancing with a girl from Amsterdam, and I had a great time.
In Amsterdam we had partied in the streets; here we danced
in the village cafés.

My mother went around renewing her friendship with
the villagers, who were all glad to see her again. I wasn't
interested in accompanying her on those visits. During
the day I went bicycling with Chantal and friends in the
countryside, and one time we visited an airfield nearby,
where we were taken up for a spin in an old warplane. My
very first time flying.

I went to the churchyard with my mother and Albert to visit
my grandparents' grave. Now the headstone was engraved
with 'Leonie' and 'Jérôme,' underneath the name of 'Notre
petit René'.

'Whatever *did* happen to René?' I asked my mother. I had
never asked about it before.

She now told me that her sister Yvette had caused her own
child to drown. Yvette would frequently fly off the handle,

and she was unreasonably jealous. After a furious fight with her husband, she had run off to her parents' house. Then, somewhere close to the village, she had jumped into the Seine with her child. Onlookers had managed to pull Yvette out of the water, but the baby had been beyond rescue. I also gathered from the way my mother told the story that my sister and I might never have been born had it not been for the death of that child.

But I had done a rather poor job of replacing our deceased cousin; of that I was sure.

My mother decided it was high time to modernise the house. It had taken a long time for gas, electricity and municipal water to come to the village, but once it had, my grandfather had resisted. 'I'm not going to let them make holes in my house,' he'd said, and no one had dared to go against his wishes. My mother had just left it that way, even though the house was hers, not his. So Albert went on fetching water from the pump down the street, and my grandmother continued making the most delicious concoctions on a wood stove in the kitchen.

One of the fruit orchards belonging to my father was sold. My parents could use the money. Part of the profit was put towards my mother's share of the roof repair and the installation of the gas, electricity and water.

My grandfather's vegetable garden was not sold; Albert liked to work in it. That was fine with Eline. As far as she was concerned, he could have anything he wanted. She still considered him her little brother.

17

Before taking the train from Paris back to Amsterdam, we paid a visit to Aunt Julie. I did not know her. She was my grandfather's sister, and an outcast in the family. But my mother thought it was time to bury the family feud. Julie's husband was dead, my grandparents were dead, and the aunt was now an old lady and very rich to boot. She received us in her apartment and greeted us in a cool, though not unfriendly, manner. Champagne was served, with madeleines. I did not like champagne, but my mother, who was aware of that, sent me a look of warning, and I forced myself to swallow the foamy liquid.

She had warned me ahead of time to take care not to make any mistakes in French, because that might not go down well here. I had already gathered that for some reason or another it was important that I make a good impression. But the effect of my mother's words of warning was that I didn't dare open my mouth at all. Nor did I have the foggiest idea what I was supposed to talk about with this aunt; and anyway, once she had greeted me, she didn't talk to me again. I did not listen to the conversation between the two adults and occupied myself instead with her two Pekinese, who had first growled on approaching the new visitors, but later, after I'd fed them my madeleine, let me pet them and came to lie at my feet.

I looked round at the art in the room, and noticed the fans displayed in gilt cases, as well as the paintings and prints hanging on the wall. Some of these depicted pastoral scenes of elegantly dressed ladies and men in fine costumes in amorous dalliance, being spied on by impish little cupids hiding in the bushes.

Suddenly I heard Julie say, 'You have only yourself to blame for the trials you suffered in the war. You know that your father was against your marriage in the first place. And Damien wasn't very pleased about it either, even though he did help you out during the war.'

I knew that an uncle of my mother's, a collaborator, had provided the papers that had saved our lives, and I pricked up my ears. Julie went on, 'And now they're driving round in their big fancy automobiles again, if you please!'

I saw my mother's mouth open to give her a piece of her mind, as she always did when faced with that sort of remark. She did not share my timidity in these matters. But, quite uncharacteristically, she shut her mouth again, and sighed.

I brooded that my father didn't ride around in a fancy car at all. On the contrary, he had lost everything in the war, including all of his relatives. The uncle and aunt I had so liked to stay with, my cousins who had been my playmates, they were all gone.

Abruptly Aunt Julie turned and stared at me, and said harshly, in broken German, 'So, you don't speak any French at all? But your mother is French!'

The dogs were startled from their slumber and scurried to their basket in a corner of the room.

I turned bright red and started stammering, not knowing

whether to answer in German or in French. My mother came to the rescue by glancing at the clock on the fireplace mantel and saying we'd have to hurry if were going to make our train.

It was the first and also the last time I saw Aunt Julie. Six months later she was dead.

I had expected to be berated for my awkward behaviour during the visit, but my mother did not mention it. Instead she told me the story of Julie. She was not in the habit of confiding in me or discussing risqué subjects with me; that was reserved for my sister, but this time she was in an expansive mood, probably because she had had to restrain herself so in the previous hours.

Julie, the posh lady in her beautiful apartment, had been the mistress of a prominent, wealthy man. It was he who had bought the apartment she still lived in, and upon his death he had left her a good part of his fortune. The money was well invested in stocks and property, and when some years later she married Damien, she had already made herself a small fortune. Since the war their holdings had appreciated considerably, in no little way owing to the fact that their relationship with the people in power during the war had proved very fruitful. Her husband no longer enjoyed the benefits, however, since he had passed away suddenly at the end of the war. My mother could not or would not give me a satisfactory explanation for the cause of his death. But her reticence on the matter made me suspect that it had something to do with the French Resistance's radical methods in dealing with collaborators in the chaotic months following liberation. In the summer of 1944 the Resistance had taken justice into its own hands, since the slow pace of the justice system and De Gaulle's liberal amnesty policy failed to satisfy their bitter lust for vengeance. It had led to total anarchy and bloodshed.

Julie had a nickname in the family too: *La Putain*, the whore.

So there was a cautious rapprochement between Julie and my mother, and a few months after we visited her, Aunt Julie wrote her a letter in which she asked her niece to come to her because she was dying. My mother left for Paris at once to be at her aunt's side in her final days and to stake a claim to the inheritance on behalf of her brother and herself. When six weeks later Julie had not yet died, Eline turned to her brother, who still refused to have anything to do with his aunt. 'It was bad enough that during the war I had to contact that collaborator for you, while I was with the Resistance,' he said. But in the end she did manage to convince him to take over from her in caring for the aunt, since she did not want to spend any more time away from Amsterdam, and Julie might still make a will favouring her late husband's family, something my mother wished to forestall at all costs. She did not tell him that her relationship with her aunt was about to fall to pieces because it was getting harder and harder for her to keep the aunt's wartime past and the opinions that went with it out of the conversation.

Reluctantly Albert reconciled with his aunt, who died three weeks later. She left him her entire fortune.

Albert mentioned this last bit of information in passing, in a postscript at the end of the letter announcing the aunt's death. It gave rise to enormous consternation in Amsterdam. My parents had lost a lot of money in the war and my mother had been counting on receiving a portion of the inheritance. She believed that half of the inheritance ought to be hers, because she had been the one to make Albert reconcile with his aunt. Albert was not of the same mind, it seemed, because he did not say a word about it in his letter.

She decided a few months later to visit him, in order to see how things stood. But she returned home just a few days later. When I came home from school that afternoon, she and my father were having lunch. They were in the midst of an intense conversation. I noticed all of a sudden how the hard war years had left their mark on both of their faces. My father's health had deteriorated. Nobody else in his family had survived the war. From the moment he had received final confirmation of this, he had avoided the subject, but my mother knew very well that he needed her and her optimistic outlook to be able to go on living with that loss. I gathered that her trip had been for nought. She had quarrelled with her brother about the upkeep of the house, which he had let fall into disrepair; he thought she should be the one responsible for fixing it up. He was quite conscious of the fact that her post-war financial situation was no longer all that rosy. I gathered that Albert, now that he had become the one with all the money, was using the power that this lent him to lord it over his sister; he wanted to show that he would no longer be patronised by her. She had left abruptly in order not to pour any more oil on the fire, because he had mentioned in passing that he would arrange things to her satisfaction all in good time, and that her daughters would eventually be his heirs. So it was a matter of remaining on friendly terms with her brother.

'You must understand why Aunt Julie did not leave anything to me,' she said to me. I understood only all too well. When we had visited her, Aunt Julie had not tried to hide her anti-Semitic feelings. And my bashfulness and poor command of French can't have helped either.

My mother's relationship with her brother was never restored to what it once was. Albert made it clear that he no longer considered her as one of them. She did not return to the village again herself, but she did encourage me to visit him on a regular basis. Jeanne had had three wishes when Albert came into the inheritance: a black astrakhan fur coat, a handbag of crocodile leather, and diamond earrings. Albert had given her the three things she coveted, and she was quite content to live in the poorly-maintained house. Apparently her living conditions didn't matter to her. I never told my mother about the deplorable state the house was in, and she never asked. Twenty years would go by before we went to the village together once more, to attend Albert's funeral. He had died unexpectedly. It was the last time she ever went there.

This unpleasant business cast a pall over the rest of her life, and caused her to become estranged from the land of her birth. The upshot of this was that she did finally come to appreciate the habits and customs of the Dutch, which she had always been so critical of before.

My mother had lost the inheritance, but she wasn't the type to let something like that keep her down. I am sure that the minute she rushed to board that train back to Amsterdam, she was already thinking about the future. She would simply continue to work as a seamstress, the skill that had helped her provide for her entire family during the war years. She would not let Albert get her down.

When she arrived at Amsterdam's Central Station, as she crossed the square heading for a telephone booth, she noticed that the herring cart that she had seen at the other side of the bridge on her first visit to Amsterdam over thirty years before was in business again; until the outbreak of war, that cart had always been in that same spot. In the intervening years she had learned to appreciate the taste of *Hollandse nieuwe*, the raw pickled herring so beloved by the Dutch. It gave her an idea.

PART THREE

Hijman

1

Hijman awoke. He had been dreaming. A room full of people. He saw his brother Arie standing in the corner, with his back turned to him. He had pushed his way through the crowd laboriously, but when he finally managed to reach Arie, he had vanished and when he looked round, he saw that the room was empty. He was all alone. Hijman lay in bed thinking about his dream, and could not shake the feeling of loneliness that overcame him.

He had returned from the Achterhoek region in the eastern part of the country the previous day. The Jewish community there had been so severely reduced that they had difficulty gathering the quorum of ten men needed for worship. For certain services, men from other parts of the country were invited to round out the numbers for the *minyan*. He had been the guest, for a few days, of an orthodox Jewish family.

He knew quite well how he had come to dream such a dream. His host had returned from Auschwitz after the war. He had his camp number tattooed on his arm. He had taken Hijman aside on the last night. 'I've never told anyone,' he had said, 'not even my wife, but I have to tell someone. Someone had to do the dirty work. I did the dirty work. I was the one who dragged the bodies out of the gas chambers and brought them to the crematorium. I was ordered to remove the gold rings and gold teeth first. I would have done anything to save my life. I was estranged from all humanity. Those ovens, that image is with me day and night.'

Hijman always did his best not to think about the hell that had been the concentration camp where his brothers, his sisters and their children had ended up. But this confession made them come uppermost in his mind again, and with renewed intensity. What the man had told him had shaken him badly. In the train on the way home he could think of nothing else. Arie, whose friendship he missed so much. Martha, his favourite sister. To connect them with this hideous method of extermination was simply unbearable.

When, with his co-religionists, he had triumphantly returned the scrolls to the main synagogue a few days after the liberation, he had still been hoping for their return. But now, more than two years later, he knew that he would never see his family or most of his friends again.

It was quiet in the house. Eline had gone to Paris. His daughters had already gone out. He had arranged to meet his youngest daughter that afternoon after school, to scout locations where he might open a print shop. The war had left him in such poor health that he no longer had the wherewithal to start his import business from scratch again. He had now taken up his hobby of dealing in old books and prints once more, which had also been his occupation at the start of the war, before the Germans robbed him of the means to pursue it. Before she left, Eline had suggested that he open a shop selling old prints.

His youngest daughter was just as eager as he was to skirt any conversations about the war or the deported relatives. She, too, never talked about it. Eline, in particular, did not understand this – she who never had any compunction about expressing her feelings. Their friend Otto, who had lost his wife and both daughters, wanted to talk about his daughter Anne, with her. But the girl was not prepared to do so, at least not at home. That was why he often took her out for the evening; then they would talk about her friendship with Anne and about the diary Anne had written and which had been published a few months earlier. When she came home from one of these sessions with Otto, she usually wouldn't say a word, and would go straight up to bed.

Eline and Hijman didn't understand their youngest daughter at all any more, and had less and less interaction with her. She seemed to feel no emotion whatsoever over the loss of her cousins and friends. She never talked about it. Otto Frank had shown Eline and Hijman the passages in his daughter's diary in which she mentioned her friendship with their daughter, and it had surprised them both. Anne had written some remarkable things in there. They could see how close the girls' friendship had been. But Hijman's daughter refused to read the diary.

During the past school year she had applied herself diligently to pass her fourth year at the lyceum with flying colours. She had been planning to switch to the arts and crafts school the following year. But, encouraged by the stellar report card, and on the insistent advice of her elders, she had now been convinced to finish the lyceum instead. It was great for her self-confidence, but Hijman thought it was a pity. He had never been given the chance to develop his own artistic talents. He would have loved to live as an artist, but in his time, in the little world in which he once lived, it had been out of the question. He now hoped that his daughter would not abandon her original ambition completely, and that by the time that she was ready for it, they would still be able to finance her art studies.

He turned on the radio. The news came on, announcing that the General Assembly of the United Nations had proposed the creation of a Jewish state in Palestine. It seemed like a dream. After centuries of persecution, the Jews would be returning to the 'promised land'. They would be able to continue the work of reclaiming the desert and draining the swamps. It would once again become the 'land of milk and honey' that it had been in ages past.

He got out of bed and began to get dressed.

2

Too many books checked off again, he thought to himself as he pushed aside the auction catalogue. The telephone rang. It was Robert, inviting him to go sailing with him on the Zuider Zee the next day.

Hijman turned down the invitation. 'I couldn't possibly come,' he said. 'Tomorrow is the auction's viewing day.'

'Can't I make you change your mind?' Robert attempted, 'It's the first time since the winter that we're taking the boat out.'

'I can't bid on a book I haven't inspected first,' said Hijman.

'Hijman, you've got to help me. That French woman, the one I introduced you to last week at the Concertgebouw, has to be entertained. She is worth her weight in gold to our firm, and we have to make sure she doesn't miss Paris too much. Otherwise she'll be gone before you know it. You speak French fluently – in fact, she thought you were French! And I couldn't help noticing you were a little disappointed afterwards when you saw she was no longer with us.'

'Right, but where had she gone off to, then?' asked Hijman, who had indeed been charmed by Eline.

'Fie Carelsen and Pisuisse, you know, the actors, had offered to take her home. They live near her, on the Leidsekade.'

'I'll come,' said Hijman. 'But at the risk of buying a pig in a poke at the auction!'

Eline and Hijman spent all the next day in each other's company. The weather was gorgeous, and they sailed to Volendam, where she had her first taste of smoked eel. She looked splendid in her casual crêpe de Chine outfit. Her gaiety and witty conversation amused him, and he was determined not to lose sight of her again. When they arrived back at Muiden, he invited her to have dinner with him the next night.

On the boat they had discussed Sarah Bernhardt, the French actress of Dutch-Jewish background whom she had seen perform in *L'Aiglon* in Paris. It had been one of the great actress's starring roles. At Monday's book auction he'd had no problem acquiring the books he had checked off in the catalogue for his collection, and he'd also bought Eline a beautiful leather-bound copy of Edmond Rostand's *L'Aiglon*. He told her that the piece, under the title *The Eaglet*, had also been acclaimed in Holland when it had played there.

He brought her the book that night, and she told him about Paris and about her parents. She made it clear to him that she did not intend to remain in Amsterdam permanently, and he realised he'd have to move quickly if he wanted to capture Eline for himself.

She wanted to know all about the Jewish religion and Jewish customs, of which she knew nothing.

He decided he would take her to meet his parents right

away. That would make them see that it was time for them to stop trying to pair him up with his childhood playmate Clara. Having lived abroad, he felt he had outgrown his parental milieu, and when he returned from Paris upon his father's urgent insistence a year earlier, he had taken rooms on Plantage Parklaan.

He had chosen a Sabbath evening for her introduction to the family, which they took as a sign that he was serious about her. All the siblings usually came home for Friday-night supper; even his sister Greta had come all the way from The Hague with her husband and two little girls, for she was curious to meet her brother's new girlfriend.

Eline received a rather cool welcome from his father and mother; they had something else in mind for their son. His mother had dreaded meeting this French girlfriend of his. They thought it strange that she called him by the name Armand, and since she barely spoke any Dutch, they could not have a meaningful conversation. But Eline did have a nice chat with Hijman's brother Arie, and Martha, the youngest sister, who were the only members of the family who spoke French. Both of them congratulated him on his catch.

Hijman wanted to ask Eline to marry him. But still he held back. How would he persuade her to remain in Amsterdam? She was so attached to the city of her birth. In the short time since he had settled back in Amsterdam, he had managed to expand his agency and commission business in partnership with his brother Arie, and at the request of his father had also taken his brother Jacques, the gadabout of the family, into the business. Jacques had enthusiastically resumed his accounting studies.

One evening, when Eline showed him the contract she had been offered, Hijman proposed that she remain in

Amsterdam and marry him. She would be able to keep her present job and she would be travelling to Paris for business on a regular basis.

'No,' said Eline. She repeated it three times: *'Non, non, non,'* as if to persuade herself that she was making the right decision. Then she rushed out the door.

She left for Paris three days later.

3

He made up his mind during the family's annual outing to Zandvoort. His mother had doled out the sandwiches and fruit from the picnic basket, and they had drunk the coffee served to them by the beach boy. Now his parents were contentedly lounging in the wicker beach chairs that the boy had set up for them earlier: his father in his suit, his mother in her Sunday best, wearing her new hat. They had all come except for Greta, who together with her husband often worked overtime at the dry cleaner's on Sundays.

Hijman had asked Clara to marry him the month before. His parents had been visibly relieved when Eline had suddenly departed for Paris, and Hijman had stopped talking about her. They had seized their chance, and he had given in, listening to their argument that Clara, their best friends' daughter, was the right woman for him to marry and start a family with.

In the train to Zandvoort, however, Hijman had suddenly known it beyond a doubt. He could not marry Clara if his thoughts were constantly with Eline. He had already talked it over with Arie, who had advised him to break off the engagement, even if it meant earning the displeasure of both families. 'I can keep the business going in Amsterdam as your partner, while you run it from Paris.'

His two younger brothers strolled off together after lunch. Jacques had spotted two girls he knew on the beach, sitting a little farther off with their parents. His father was shaking the sand out of his shoes, and his mother was peeling an apple.

Hijman caught Arie's eye, as he was talking to Martha in the sand next to the two beach chairs.

'Come,' Hijman said to Clara, 'let's go for a little walk.'

They walked along the shore without exchanging a word.

Clara broke the silence between them. 'What's the matter?' she asked. 'Why don't you say something?'

Then he explained to her that there could never really be anything between them.

At first she reacted angrily. 'It might have been better if you had come to that conclusion before we were engaged,' she said.

But a little later she burst into tears. She said she wanted to go back to Amsterdam at once.

He took her to the train. When he proposed to accompany her, she said, 'I'd rather go home alone. You'd better go and explain to your parents why I left.'

He walked back to the beach from the station. He was unhappy with himself. Clara was right, of course. By allowing himself to be influenced by his parents, he had caused her pain and had not done himself any favours.

Arie saw him approach from the top of the dunes. He pulled his sister up from the sand by the arm. 'Martha and I are going for a walk, Father,' Hijman heard him say.

'Where is Clara?' asked his mother, when Hijman came up to them.

'I took her to the train,' he said. 'Our engagement is off. I'm leaving for Paris tomorrow.'

Before they had stopped writing to each other, Eline had sent him her new address.

As he was ringing her doorbell, she was just walking up the street. She was flabbergasted. Before she could open her mouth to speak, he said, 'We're going to get married. I'm going to do my business from Paris.'

Hastily she opened the door and pulled him into the hall. 'The neighbours,' she said, 'they're nosy.' She wouldn't let him take her in his arms until they were upstairs.

She agreed right away to convert to Judaism and to go to the rabbi for instruction. 'For the sake of the children we're going to have some day,' he said. 'They can't be Jewish unless their mother is Jewish.' But she remained vague when it came to having children. Still, he knew how important her work was to her, and did not want to importune her further on the subject for the time being.

He accompanied her to the village where her parents lived. A kind mother, who was also a very good cook. Eline had warned him beforehand that her father might act rather cool towards him, and not to let it bother him; but Hijman found him an interesting fellow, and Eline was surprised to see that they got along so well and seemed to have so many mutual interests.

And yet Hijman had found it troubling when the topic of Emile Zola and Alfred Dreyfus came up, and he realised that his father-in-law had firmly believed in the guilt of the Jew, Dreyfus. But he did not let the discussion get out of hand. He was only too aware that the captain had received little support from his co-religionists at the time. It had been over a hundred years since the Revolution, the Jews had become integrated in liberal, tolerant France and held top positions in government and academia. 'Freedom, equality, fraternity' was the motto. With the exception of a few loyal supporters, like Dreyfus's brother Mathieu, the Baron de Rothschild and the chief rabbi of Paris, they had kept themselves aloof from this controversy; they preferred to consider it Alfred Dreyfus's private affair, and thought it was a matter that did not concern them. Not until Emile Zola's article led to an outbreak of anti-Semitism did they stick out their necks and declare whose side they were on. It was also then that Marcel Proust, who used to frequent the salons of the *anti-Dreyfusards*, revealed that he himself was of Jewish origin, writing in a letter to one of his friends: 'I did not reply yesterday to your question about the Jews, and for this simple reason: even though I am Catholic like my father and brother, my mother, on the other hand, is Jewish. You will understand that this is sufficient reason for me to abstain from this type of discussion.'

On that first day Hijman also met Eline's brother Albert. After his failed marriage, he had moved in with his parents again. His sister had had him in mind as well when she had bought the house, because the healthy air of the forest in the hills above Paris did his weak lungs a world of good. In the meantime he had acquired a new girlfriend, Jeanne, whom he brought to the village on one occasion. His mother had called her *une bonne fille*, a good girl, but his father and Eline couldn't understand what he saw in her. They didn't find her very interesting, and had made no bones about it. Jeanne didn't come back to the village after that one visit.

They now spent every Sunday in the village, and Hijman was soon accepted into the small village community.

He had not counted on his parents travelling to Paris

for the wedding, even though he had told them that they would be married in a synagogue. His parents were not happy about his choice and did not try to hide it. But for Eline, it had the advantage of not having to explain to her parents that she had converted. She just told them that they had decided on a quiet civil wedding, with Arie and Albert acting as witnesses.

Their honeymoon took them to Garmisch-Partenkirchen, where Hijman used to spend winter vacations when he lived in Germany with his parents. Eline sat out on the terrace as Hijman demonstrated his skiing proficiency.

He told her about his youth in Frankfurt, and how his family had ended up there at the close of the nineteenth century.

4

Hijman had spent less than ten years of his youth in Amsterdam. His father had been a diamond cutter there, earning enough at first to feed his family of six. But, because of the Boer War in South Africa, diamond imports dried up, and many workers in the diamond trade were laid off, his father among them. It was all the more dire because there was a fifth baby on the way. His father decided to take an acquaintance living in Frankfurt up on the suggestion of going into the egg business with him.

Hijman remembered quite clearly the first time that he and his mother, his little sister and his brothers had arrived in Frankfurt. The family had stayed behind in Amsterdam until the new baby was born, while his father had made preparations for their arrival in their new German home.

'Papa, you're crying,' he had said at the Frankfurt railway station, when his father had seen his six-week-old baby for the first time.

He had found them an apartment on Mainstrasse, in a neighbourhood still largely populated by Jews, although the ghetto had been abolished at the beginning of the nineteenth century. In 1860 a large synagogue had been built there on the Börneplatz, partially financed by Anselm Rothschild, the patriarch of the banking dynasty.

The thing Hijman especially appreciated about this neighbourhood was the fact that it bordered the Main River. In Amsterdam his home had been near the Amstel River. So the river gave him a sense both of familiarity and of distance – the option of either staying home, or of leaving home.

He already began feeling the urge to leave while in secondary school, to get away from the closed Frankfurt society, with its restrictive rules. Again and again he was drawn to the river near his home, with its promise of a wide-open future.

His father did not object when after finishing school Hijman told them that he wanted to go abroad. He didn't want to go on with his studies, nor did he want to work in his father's firm, which had since grown into a flourishing chemical import and export business. He wanted to travel, to explore the world.

In order to earn money for his future travels, Hijman worked for a bookbinder on Mainstrasse in his spare time. That experience had turned him into a bibliophile, and it was what eventually spurred him to become a book collector.

A week after passing his finals, Hijman boarded a ship for England with fifty guilders in his pocket. He worked in Birmingham for six months. Then, deciding he knew sufficient English, he sailed to France.

In Calais he worked for an importer of Scottish tweeds and British worsted. He didn't care about the salary, all that mattered to him was to learn French. He would jot down in a little notebook any new French words that he came across, and at night he would look them up in the dictionary.

He was quickly promoted and became the firm's sales representative for France and Germany.

But the outbreak of World War I put a stop to all this. His family returned from Frankfurt to Amsterdam, and he too came back to the Netherlands, which remained neutral in the war. He began working for his father, who had started a business in colonial goods and spices. His brother Arie also worked in the family business.

As soon as the war was over, however, Hijman left for Paris. He wanted to go his own way. His parents did not understand his interest in art and culture. They couldn't stand seeing him spending good money on old books and prints, and they were appalled to hear how much he had spent on a valuable coin for his coin collection.

He changed his name to Armand, and although he did not try to hide his Jewish background, and had many Jewish friends in Paris, he stopped practising his religion – much to his parents' dismay. There had been several, blatant attempts to fix him up with girls in their circle of friends as suitable marriage prospects. They did the same with Arie, but neither of the brothers had taken the bait; on the contrary, in Hijman's case it had pushed him to leave Amsterdam as soon as he could.

In Paris he got a job working for a fabric wholesaler. He rented rooms on the Rue de Richelieu, close to the Bibliothèque Nationale, where he could often be found poring over old books in his spare time. He also plunged into the Paris nightlife. The war was over, and the mood was one of optimism and gaiety. He went with friends and acquaintances to the *cafés-chantants* to listen to popular singers and songstresses. He attended performances at the Opéra and the Opéra Comique. At the Comédie Française he was introduced to the dramas of classical French literature.

His brother Arie frequently came to stay with him in Paris.

During one of those visits, in the mid-1920s, Arie shared with him his concerns over his parents.

'They're growing old,' he said, 'Father's asthma is getting worse. I'm afraid he'll have to stop working soon. On top of that, Jacques is a great source of worry to them; he refuses to study, and can't seem to keep a job.'

'Do you mean that you think I should return to Amsterdam?' asked Hijman.

'Yes, that is what I mean,' replied Arie.

Why did he give in to his brother's wish so easily? He felt torn – torn between the ties that bound him to his family and his urge to escape.

He packed his bags and returned to Amsterdam.

5

When Hijman was dressed, he hastily drained a cup of coffee and went out the door. He had to hurry. There were nine men waiting for him.

On the way to the synagogue his thoughts were with Eline. He was still in awe of her energy and her vigour, to which he and his daughters owed their lives. But at the same time it irked him to be constantly reminded of it, even though they never talked about it any more. It had affected their relationship, and the slightest argument these days turned into a raging quarrel. Whenever that happened, he would clam up and stalk out of the house to meet the few friends who had also survived the war. With a handful of them who, like him, had been safe from deportation, and with some others in hiding who were able to get out and join them from time to time, he had continued to observe his faith throughout the war, strengthening his belief. Now that the war was over, they were looking to each other for support while trying to resume their normal lives.

Eline's house was always open to everyone. As always, many different people looked to her for support. She had all the time in the world for them, and especially for those who had been left behind as the sole survivor. She'd make them a quick cup of coffee or a bowl of soup, and for those who came at mealtimes she would dash out to the fishmongers's on Rijn Street for a piece of fish. French friends of hers who lived in Amsterdam also visited often, for example, the manager of a fabric shop on Kalver Street. 'You'll see, we'll both end up in the Zorgvlied cemetery some day,' he once said to Eline, meaning that he, too, having spent the war years in Holland, had outgrown his fatherland. And on Tuesday evenings the same two people were always there for dinner: a violinist and a poetess.

But Eline did not participate in Hijman's orthodox Jewish religious and cultural practice. This had given rise to an even greater wedge between them. The strong bond that had brought them together, through their shared interest in art and beautiful things, was now gone, and their utterly different personalities and backgrounds had begun taking their toll.

Still, he missed her, now that she wasn't home. He missed the ability she had never to look back, but always to stay focused on the future.

When he came home an hour later, the telephone rang. Eline told him that she had just arrived at the Central Station.

'I'm taking a taxi home,' she said. 'But first I'm going to buy some herring for our lunch.' Her voice sounded upbeat.

'I'll put the coffee on,' he said.

Acknowledgements and Thanks

The extracts from the diaries of Anne Frank were taken from *The Diaries of Anne Frank*, published by the Rijksinstituut voor Oorlogsdocumentatie (RIOD, Royal Institute of War Documentation), Amsterdam 1986.

The photographs numbered 11 and 12 are from the RIOD.

The photograph of Anne Frank and the documents numbered 14 and 22 are from the Anne Frank Institute.

All other photographs and documents are from Jacqueline van Maarsen's private collection.

I would like to thank my sister Christiane, who was at times able to supplement my memories with her own.

My thanks also go to Ruud, my husband and never-abating support.

I would also like to thank my publisher Wil Hansen, who managed to draw much more out of me than I thought I had in me.

L'Oréal Took My Home: The Secrets of a Theft

Monica Waitzfelder

'L'Oréal took my home,' Edith Rosenfelder was always saying. This claim affected her daughter Monica, who decided when she grew up she'd try to understand what lay behind it. It was the start of a true investigation leading to action in the French courts. Prior to 1937, Monica Waitzfelder's family lived in Germany. Being Jewish, they were forced to flee the country, abandoning all their possessions, and their property was looted in the same way as happened to many other European Jews, who were victims of persecution prior to the Holocaust.

This is the story of how the Rosenfelder family never recovered their house, which was located in the centre of Karlsruhe, Germany. It was a wonderful location in which the L'Oréal cosmetics firm opened its head office. It refused – and refuses – to recognise the legitimate owners.

Praise for *L'Oréal Took My Home*

'A meticulously documented thriller worthy of Forsyth or Grisham'
– *New Statesman*

'France's richest resident, cosmetics heiress Liliane Bettencourt […] is fending off allegations of ugly behaviour by her father, L'Oréal founder and alleged Nazi sympathiser Eugene Schueller…*L'Oréal Took My Home* details [the family's] fight with L'Oréal, replete with detailed documentation'
– *Forbes magazine*

'It is right that this book should be published.
It is a painful story, passionately told and fully documented,
of the forcible appropriation of the home of a Jewish family by
the Nazis in 1938, which finally came into the possession of the
cosmetics giants, L'Oréal' – Baroness Mary Warnock, DBE

'[L'Oréal] played a part in the loss of Waitzfelder's
family home. Shocking too, to read of the early days of L'Oréal –
something to remember when you are next shampooing your hair.
It still reverberates' – Top Titles, *Publishing News*

Also available from Arcadia Books

Parallel Lines

Peter Lantos

His is a story of a young boy's journey from a sleepy provincial town
in Hungary during the Second World War to the concentration camp
in Bergen-Belsen.

Unlike other books dealing with this period, this is not a Holocaust story, but a
child's recollection of a journey full of surprise, excitement, bereavement and
terror. Yet this remains a testimony of survival, overcoming obstacles which to
adults may seem insurmountable but to a child were just part of an adventure
and, ultimately, recovery. After having established a career in the West, the
author decided to revisit the stages of his earlier journeys, reliving the past
through the perspective of the present. Along the way, ghosts from the past
are finally laid to rest by the kindness of new friends.

Praise for *Parallel Lines*

'The most heartening part of this movingly narrated memoir is the
regenerative spirit shown by the survivors. It is difficult to take in the
enormity of the worst European atrocity of the last century, which is why
one person's experience brings it home more fully – particularly when that
person is a child for whom the terrible experience was also an adventure'
– *The Independent*

'Reminds us that the end of the war was by no means the end of hardship,
entailing further resilience. I defy anyone to read this account without
retrospective anger on behalf of those who suffered' – *Jewish Chronicle*

'Anyone who thinks they have read all there is to be said about the Holocaust
should read one more book, *Parallel Lines*. A child's clear-eyed journey to hell
paralleled by an adult's scientific quest to understand that journey'
– Anne Sebba, author of *The Exiled Collector*

The Twins

Tessa de Loo

Two sisters, Lotte and Anna, share a bond that is far stronger than anyone except they alone can understand. But when war comes between them, the two discover that even the deepest bonds have their limits.

Historical and human perspectives clash in this cool, compassionate psychological novel centred around the 1990 chance meeting of two elderly women at Spa, the Belgian health resort. Each woman has come for the famously curative waters. But not by chance does each suffer from debilitating arthritis. The women are twins, separated in childhood by the death of their parents. Anna stays in their native Germany, while Lotte is taken in by relatives in the Netherlands. Consequently, they lose touch with each other and live through the rise of Hitler, the Second World War and the post-war era from opposed positions. Lotte despises the Germans and feels disconnected from them, believing that in her sister's place she would have acted differently, since her husband was a Dutch Jew. Anna, meanwhile, though certainly a good woman who harbours only feelings of contempt for the Nazis, married an SS officer from Vienna. What was the degree of her complicity in Nazi horrors? Both sisters lost their husbands in the war, one to random Allied bombing, the other to an Austrian concentration camp. The narrative unfolds through a series of often thorny conversations, as the sisters probe these and other points of contention. De Loo artfully weaves two fully developed fictional personalities into an expertly realised historical background. She addresses notions of guilt and responsibility in a sensitive, thought-provoking manner, without exonerating or condemning.

Praise for The Twins

'Completely original ... takes the reader's breath away'
– Joan Smith, *Sunday Times*

'Outstanding ... women of this gallantry exist in every country but it is a rarity to find them so truly and vividly transmitted' – Nicolas Freeling

Also available from Arcadia Books

The Memory Man

Lisa Appignanesi

Winner of the 2005 Holocaust Literature Award and shortlisted for the
Commonwealth Writers' Prize. Bruno Lind is on a mission though he may
not know it. Irene Davies knows she is, but isn't sure it's the right one. Both
of them are haunted by the legacy of a tangled history of love and war.

When Bruno Lind returns to Vienna, the city of his birth, after an absence of
many years, more awaits him than his memory hinted. Yet Lind is an expert
on memory, a neuroscientist of international renown. His own story, dredged
from the past, shouldn't elude his explanatory capacities. In this poignant
novel, studded with vivid characters and rare humour, Appignanesi returns
to the terrain of her acclaimed family memoir, *Losing the Dead*. Drawing on her
intimate knowledge of Central Europe, she has created compelling fiction that
is also an exploration of mind and memory.

Praise for *The Memory Man*

'…It speaks history, and one cannot stop listening' – John Berger

'Appignanesi's stunning novel…really stayed with me'
– Helena Kennedy QC, Books of the Year, *The Guardian*

'This clever novel is loaded with symbolic touches, but it is also unexpectedly
funny, and pegs along at a thrillerish pace as Lind turns detective of his own
early life, travelling East via vanished family and lost loves' – *Daily Mail*

'A novel of big ideas. *The Memory Man* makes us question how
memories are made, and fates formed' – Gilian Slovo

'The way she intertwines past and present, nightmare and
social comedy, brutal suffering and contemporary flirtation,
is adroit and elegant. This is a book everyone will read
with horror and fascination' – Edmund White

The Last Kabbalist of Lisbon

Richard Zimler

A gripping literary mystery in the tradition of *The Name of the Rose*, set among secret Jews living in Lisbon in the sixteenth century.

The year is 1506, and the streets of Lisbon are seething with fear and suspicion when Abraham Zarco is found dead, a naked girl at his side. Abraham was a renowned kabbalist, a practitioner of the arcane mysteries of the Jewish tradition at a time when the Jews of Portugal were forced to convert to Christianity. Berekiah, a talented young manuscript illuminator, investigates his uncle's murder, and discovers in the kabbalah clues that lead him into the labyrinth of secrets in which Jews sought to hide from their persecutors.

Praise for *The Last Kabbalist of Lisbon*

'Remarkable erudition and compelling imagination,
an American Umberto Eco' – *The Spectator*

'Gripping, richly written and overflowing with historic detail'
– *New York Times*

'A harrowing picture of the persecution of sixteenth-century
Portuguese Jews and, in passing, an atmospheric introduction to the
hermetic Jewish tradition of kabbalah mysticism' – *The Independent on Sunday*

'Historical accuracy, the structures of a mystery,
the pace of a thriller … a fascinating novel with
a spellbinding subject matter' – *Elle*